THE
LANGUAGES
OF
TOLKIEN'S
MIDDLE-EARTH

Books by Ruth S. Noel

*The Mythology of
Middle-earth*

*The Languages of
Tolkien's Middle-earth*

RUTH S. NOEL

THE
LANGUAGES
OF
TOLKIEN'S
MIDDLE-EARTH

BOSTON

HOUGHTON MIFFLIN COMPANY

For information about permission to reproduce
selections from this book, write to Permissions,
Houghton Mifflin Company, 215 Park Avenue South,
New York, New York 10003.

Visit our Web site: www.houghtonmifflinbooks.com.

Library of Congress Cataloging-in-Publication Data
Noel, Ruth S.
The languages of Tolkien's Middle-earth.
Edition of 1974 published under title:
The languages of Middle-earth.
"The Tolkien Dictionary": p.
I. Tolkien, John Ronald Reuel, 1892–1973
—Languages—Glossaries, etc. 2. Imaginary
languages in literature.
I. Title.
PR6039.032Z715 1980 828'.1209 80-11202
ISBN 0-395-29129-1   ISBN 0-395-29130-5 (pbk.)

Printed in the United States of America

VB

A version of this book was published by Mirage Press,
Baltimore, under the title *The Languages of Middle-earth.* The Tengwar and Angerthas letters, as drawn by
J.R.R. Tolkien, originally appeared in his *The Return
of the King,* © 1965 by J.R.R. Tolkien, and are used
by the kind permission of the publishers, George Allen
& Unwin Ltd. and Houghton Mifflin Company.

᛬ᚾᛖᛗᚾᛟᛁᛚᚨᛋᛁᚠᚨ᛬

᛬ᚦᛁᛋ᛬ᛒᚨᚠᚠᚺ᛬ᛁᛋ᛬ᚾᛖᛗᚾᛟᛁᛚᚨ᛬ᛏᛖᚾᚾ᛬ᛋᚨᚠ᛬

᛬ᚠᛚᛚ᛬ᚦᛁᛗ᛬ᚲᛗᛖᚲᛟᛗ᛬

᛬ᚹᚾᚠ᛬ᚾᚠᚢᛏ᛬ᛗᛁᛁᚠᚢᚱᚠᚷᛗᚾ᛬

᛬ᛁᛏᛋ᛬ᚠᚱᛁᛏᚾᛁᚷ᛬

᛬ᚠᛏᚾ᛬ᚦᛖᛋᛗ᛬ᚹᚾᚠ᛬ᚦᛁᛚᛚ᛬ᚠᚱᛁᛏᛏᛗ᛬ᛗᛗ᛬

᛬ᚦᛁᛒ᛬ᛁᚠᚾᚾᛗᛁᛏᛋ᛬ᛁᚠᚱᚱᛗᛁᛏᛁᚠᛏᛋ᛬ᚠᛁᚾ᛬

᛬ᛁᚠᚱᚱᛗᚺᚲᚨᛏᚾᛗᛁᛁᛗ᛬

᛬ᛁᛏ᛬ᛁᚠᚱᛖᛁᛏᚷᛁᚠᛏ᛬ᛋᛁᚱᛁᚲᛏ᛬

᛬ᛁᛏ᛬ᛗᛏᚷᛁᛋᚻ᛬ᚱᚨᛏᚷᚢᚠᚷᛗ᛬

᛬ᚠᛏᚾ᛬ᛚᛗᚷᛁᛒᛚᚨ᛬

          ᛬ᚱᚢᚦ᛬ᛏᛟᛚ᛬

Contents

PART I

LANGUAGE
IN
TOLKIEN'S
MIDDLE-EARTH

Tolkien the Linguist

The perception of order in chaos is a function of linguistics, as it is of all sciences. At rare times the development of order becomes an act of creation pure and simple. It was so when J. R. R. Tolkien produced, out of his vocation and avocation of linguistics, the literature of Middle-earth: *The Silmarillion, The Hobbit,* and *The Lord of the Rings.*

Language is so integral to culture that a linguist can reconstruct a culture from its language just as a biologist can reconstruct an animal from a bone. Tolkien's production of the invented language called Quenya compelled him to depict the Elvish cultures of *The Silmarillion.*

Tolkien spent much of his youth involved in learning, studying, and creating languages. His mother introduced him to Latin, French, and German. While at school he was taught or taught himself Greek, Middle English, Old English (also called Anglo-Saxon), Old Norse (also called Old Icelandic), Gothic, modern and medieval Welsh, Finnish, Spanish, and Italian. Other languages of which he had a working knowledge include Russian, Swedish, Danish, Norwegian, Dutch, and Lombardic.

Perhaps the critical influence that directed Tolkien's creative genius toward the works for which he is best known occurred when, at the age of twenty-one, he read the Old English religious poem *Crist* by Cynewulf. Two lines stood out vividly:

> *Eala Earendel engla beorhtast*
> *ofer middangeard monnum sended.*
> Hail Earendel, brightest of angels,
> Above Middle-earth sent unto men.

The imagery of an angelic light sent purposefully to mankind—perhaps to give hope as a precursor of the still unseen dawn, either literal or mystical—is poetically powerful. In these two lines are three elements intrinsic to Tolkien's works: a light called Earendel, its purposeful sending to men, and the word *Middle-earth.*

Middle-earth is an ancient designation for Europe or the known world of Europeans. It is universal for peoples to see their environment, large or small, as central. Medieval English spoke of the known lands as *middel-erde* or *meddel-earth.* In Old English the word was *middangeard.* In Scandinavian mythology *Midgard* designated the world of men as opposed to the worlds of gods and giants and other unearthly places.

By the time he read the *Crist* Tolkien was probably already familiar with the medieval Icelandic *Prose Edda,* in which the Eärendil figure, called *Orentil,* was an Odysseus-like mariner. Orentil was also the name of a star—probably the Morning Star—said to have been created when the god Thor carried the mariner across a freezing river. Orentil's toe froze off in the crossing, and

Thor threw it skyward where it shone ever after.

In 1914, a year after reading the *Crist,* Tolkien wrote his first poem about Earendel, as he still spelled the name, and during the following two years began to combine the theme of Eärendil with an invented language, based on Finnish, which was to become Quenya. He began to write poetry in this language. Humphrey Carpenter records a segment of one early poem for which no translation is given (*Tolkien,* p. 76):

> *Ai lintulinda Lasselanta*
> *Pilingeve suyer nalla ganta*
> *Kuluvi ya karnevalinar*
> *V'ematte singi Eldamar.*

The poem contains the elements Eldamar and Valinor essential to *The Silmarillion.* It apparently begins with a characteristic Elvish bittersweet poignancy: "O swiftly sing of the Fall of Leaves."

The Elvish languages continued to grow and flourish, and the tales that became *The Silmarillion* began to take shape. Of these languages Tolkien said, "The 'Sindarin', a Gray-Elven language, is in fact constructed deliberately to resemble Welsh phonologically and to have a relation to High-Elven similar to that existing between British (properly so-called) and Latin. All the names in the book, and the language, are of course constructed, and not at random." The book referred to was *The Lord of the Rings,* which is not in fact a trilogy (the three books are not complete stories in themselves) and was not considered so by Tolkien.

There was another element at work in the creation of names besides that of linguistic logic. Carpenter says of Tolkien, "Often in the heat of writing he would construct a name that sounded appropriate to the character without paying more than cursory attention to its linguistic origins. Later he dismissed many of the names made in this way as 'meaningless', and he subjected others to a severe philological scrutiny in an attempt to discover *how* they could have reached their strange and apparently inexplicable form" (*Tolkien,* p. 94).

However they were created, the languages are certainly not random. They lend Tolkien's works a unique dimension of realism.

*

The story of the evolution of the languages of Middle-earth is the story of the compelling hobby of a linguistic genius. The story of the evolution of the languages *in* Middle-earth is a complex tribute to Tolkien's combined talents as linguist and storyteller.

Imagine that Tolkien had found, misfiled in a library of medieval manuscripts, the crumbling, red-bound volumes, copies of ancient copies, written in Westron, the Common Speech of the Old World, a world hardly remembered in any other written history. Imagine that Tolkien translated this Westron record with poetic sureness of sound, linguistic certainty of meaning.

At times Tolkien writes as if he had made this translation. In part he does so out of sheer love of language, the joy of lavishing things with names in numerous tongues. In part he uses this device so that the languages may tell part of the story by indicating cultural characteristics and crosscultural relationships.

This is most evident in *The Lord of the Rings,* which includes words from at least fourteen invented languages as well as actual European languages and dialects of various periods. It must be borne in mind that the actual languages are, so to speak, translations of languages of Middle-earth. To some extent this must be an explanation coined by Tolkien after the fact for his use of historic languages in a prehistoric world, but the complex interrelationship of the languages still stands.

Everything in *The Lord of the Rings* is recorded by hobbits. Nothing is told that they could not know, either by experience or by report. Several things that could not be known, such as the fate of Shelob, or the content of Arwen's final interview with her father, are purposefully not specified. This restraint from using the omniscient author's viewpoint, maintained also in *The Silmarillion,* adds much to Tolkien's realism.

Everything in *The Lord of the Rings* is recorded in the language of the hobbits, Westron. When the hobbits encounter other languages, they record them in names, speech, and song. Those parts of *The Lord of the Rings* that are in English were Westron in the hypothetical original manuscript, but Westron is not English. A few Westron words are given in the appendices (for example, *Karningul* for Rivendell and *Phurunargian* for the Dwarf-delvings of Moria), but this language remains essentially foreign to the reader.

To indicate both similarities and contrasts of other languages with Westron, once English is established in Westron's place, the other languages have to evince the relationship to the English ear. Closest are the archaic, obsolete, and dialect English words. Foreign languages such as Old Norse represent a greater distance, in time or in geography, from the hobbits' Westron.

*

In the following sections the languages of the men of Westernesse, hobbits, Rohirrim, and peoples of Rhovannion will be discussed, as well as their history as it influences the languages. Glossaries are included of Old English, Old Norse, archaic English, and related languages used by Tolkien to translate the speech of these peoples. These languages indicate the relationship of the original languages to Westron as the real world languages (such as Old English) are more or less close to Modern English. The remainder of the book is concerned with the Elvish and other invented languages of Tolkien's Middle-earth.

Westron and the Lines of the Kings

The actual Westron language goes back before the first migration of men into Beleriand, the land west of and including Lindon, and of which all but Lindon sank at the end of the First Age.

The first men learned much of the language of the Dark Elves who remained east of the Misty Mountains. Because all the languages of the Elves had a common origin, when Finrod, a king of the Noldor, discovered the first men in Beleriand, he could understand much of their speech.

The first tribes of men to enter Beleriand were the House of Beor, the House of Hador, and the People of Haleth. The Elves called them the *Atani* or *Edain,* in Quenya and Sindarin respectively, and usually reserved those words for peoples descended from those three houses. Among them were numerous renowned heroes and Elf-friends, who learned the Sindarin, or Gray-Elven language. It was spoken in the houses of their leaders, and they sometimes took names in that tongue.

Eventually, all three houses of the Edain contributed to the mortal side of the descent of the Half-Elven. Beren, who wedded Lúthien, and Rían, the mother of Tuor, were of the House of Beor. Tuor's father, Huor, had his father and mother, Galdor and Hareth, from the House of Hador and the People of Haleth respectively. Tuor wedded Idril Celebrindal, and their son was Eärendil. Eärendil wedded Elwing, daughter of Beren and Lúthien's son Dior, so that Eärendil and Elwing's sons Elrond and Elros were Half-Elven on both sides of their descent.

When the First Age ended and the Edain were granted the island Númenor as their new dwelling, their leader was Elros, Half-Elven, but chooser of mortality. The Edain still spoke their own language, perhaps a little changed with time, as well as Sindarin Elvish. In Nú-menor (Westernesse) they called their language Westron, *Adûnaic* in their own tongue.

They became great mariners and established colonies, then realms, in Middle-earth, and Westron became the language of trade, a *lingua franca,* the Common Speech of all who had dealings with the Númenoreans. However, for centuries they held the Elves and the Elven tongues in reverence. They were visited by Elves from Eldamar in the Far West. They learned the Quenya language as a lan-guage of lore and ceremony, and their kings took their royal names in it.

In the division of the Númenoreans over allegiance to the Valar, language became a political issue. Ar-Adûnak-hor was the first king to take the throne in an Adûnaic name, and the disrespect was doubled, because the name meant Lord of the West, which was formerly only the title of the Elder King of the Valar. Previous kings had taken such names as *Vardamir* (Jewel of Varda, the Queen of the

Valar) and *Amandil* (Lover of Aman, the Blessed Realm). Ar-Adûnakhor forbade the use of the Elven tongues in his hearing. His grandson, Ar-Gimilzôr, totally prohibited the use of Elven speech by Númenoreans. Nevertheless, the Faithful Númenoreans, retaining their allegiance with the West, kept the memory of the languages of the Elves.

When Númenor was flooded, the remaining Númenoreans established the realms of Arnor and Gondor in Middle-earth under the leadership of Elendil. In these kingdoms they spoke the Common Speech enriched with many Elvish words and took their royal names in Quenya and most of their other names in Sindarin, often using the names of heroes among Elves and Men of the First Age. Quenya was used in lore and ceremony as it had been in the high age of Númenor. For this reason, the English representing the Common Speech in *The Lord of the Rings* ranges from the loutish mutterings and curses of trolls and Orcs, through the dialectal nattering of the Shire's gaffers and gammers, to the formal and tradition-rich language of Gondor.

The Lines of the Kings

The following chart is provided to clarify the origins and evolution of the Westron tongue, to demonstrate the great expanses of time involved, and to show the relationships of the major peoples of Tolkien's works. It gives the lines of the kings of Gondor, Arnor, and the Mark, the kings and queens of Númenor, and their ancestors in the First Age.

The chart is organized by relative time, so that although a vertical distance does not always indicate the same time-period, persons listed on the same horizontal level are contemporaries, with the single exception of the children of Elrond. Arwen, Elrond's daughter, wedded to Aragorn Elessar and mother of Eldarion (at the bottom of the chart), was born during the reign of Valandil, Isildur's son, thirty-eight generations of Dúnedain before Aragorn.

Solid lines indicate direct descent, question marks show generations for which there are no names (for example, Faramir is the grandfather of Barahir at the bottom of the chart), and dotted lines show descent where the number of intervening generations is not known.

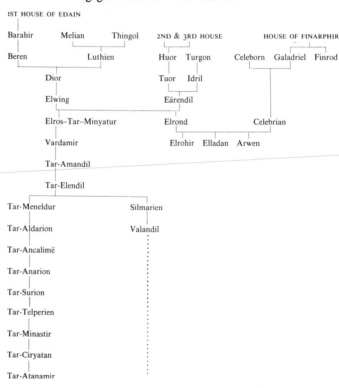

IST HOUSE OF EDAIN

Barahir   Melian   Thingol   2ND & 3RD HOUSE   HOUSE OF FINARPHIR

Beren   Luthien   Huor Turgon   Celeborn Galadriel Finrod

Dior   Tuor   Idril

Elwing   Eärendil

Elros–Tar–Minyatur   Elrond   Celebrian

Vardamir   Elrohir Elladan Arwen

Tar-Amandil

Tar-Elendil

Tar-Meneldur   Silmarien

Tar-Aldarion   Valandil

Tar-Ancalimë

Tar-Anarion

Tar-Surion

Tar-Telperien

Tar-Minastir

Tar-Ciryatan

Tar-Atanamir

Tar-Ancalimon

Tar-Telemmaite

Tar-Vanimelde

Tar-Alcarin

Tar-Calmacil

Ar-Adûnakhôr

Ar-Zimrathôn

Ar-Sakalthôr

Ar-Gimilzôr

? Ar–Inziladun (Tar-Palantir)   Amandil

Ar-Pharazôn-Tar-Miriel   Elendil

Anarion   Isildur

Meneldil   Valandil

Cemendur

Eärendil   Eldacar

Anardil

Ostoher   Arantar

Tarostar-Romendacil I   Tarcil

Turambar   Tarondor

Atanatar   Valandur

Siriondil   Elendur

Tarannon-Falastur   Tarciryan   Earendur

Eärnil   Amlaith

Ciryandil   Beleg

Ciryaher-Hyarmendacil   Mallor

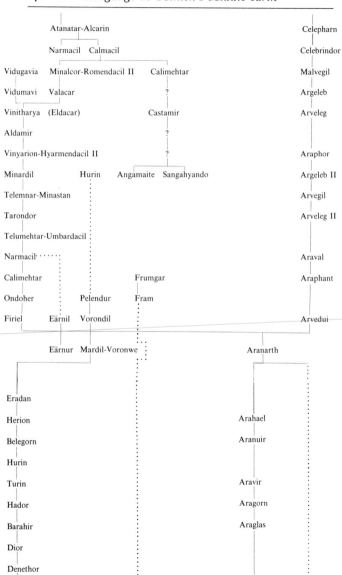

```
                Atanatar-Alcarin                                    Celepharn
                   ┌──────┴──────┐                                      │
              Narmacil       Calmacil                               Celebrindor
                           ┌──────┴──────────────────┐                  │
Vidugavia    Minalcor-Romendacil II          Calimehtar               Malvegil
   │                                                                    │
Vidumavi    Valacar                              ?                    Argeleb
   └──────┬──────┘                               │                      │
Vinitharya  (Eldacar)                        Castamir                 Arveleg
   │                                             │                      │
Aldamir                                          ?                      │
   │                                             │                      │
Vinyarion-Hyarmendacil II                        ?                   Araphor
   │                           ┌─────────────────┼──────────┐           │
Minardil                    Hurin          Angamaite   Sangahyando   Argeleb II
   │                                                                    │
Telemnar-Minastan                                                    Arvegil
   │                                                                    │
Tarondor                                                             Arveleg II
   │                                                                    │
Telumehtar-Umbardacil                                                   │
   │                                                                    │
Narmacil                                                              Araval
   │                                                                    │
Calimehtar                          Frumgar                          Araphant
   │                                    │                               │
Ondoher                    Pelendur    Fram                             │
   │                          │                                         │
Firiel       Eärnil      Vorondil                                    Arvedui
      └──────┬──────┘
          Eärnur    Mardil-Voronwe                        Aranarth
   ┌──────────┘                                      ┌───────┴───────┐
   │
Eradan                                                               │
   │                                                                 │
Herion                                            Arahael
   │                                                 │
Belegorn                                          Aranuir
   │
Hurin
   │
Turin                                             Aravir
   │                                                 │
Hador                                             Aragorn
   │                                                 │
Barahir                                           Araglas
   │
Dior
   │
Denethor
```

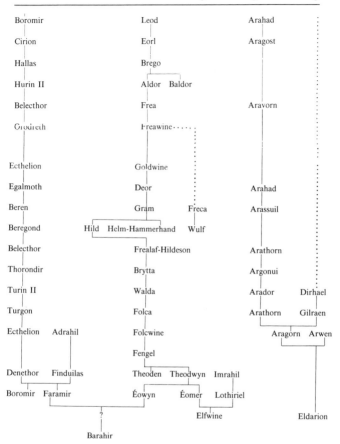

The Language
of Hobbits

The hobbits picked up their language from the people near whom they lived (see *Return of the King,* Appendix F), and although at the time of the War of the Ring the hobbits had spoken Westron for some time, they still retained important words derived from the languages of the Big Folk near whom they had lived before their migration to the Shire. These words are discussed in this section.

The Stoors of the Marish and Buckland and the Bree-land hobbits may have picked up some of their idiosyncrasies of speech from Dunlendings migrating northward into the Bree region while the Stoors still lived south near Tharbad.

A people's isolation often makes their language take divergent paths, producing dialects and, at times, separate languages. In the Marish (its own name is an old word for Marsh) the hobbits spoke a dialect and retained old words, such as *worriting.*

Place names in the Shire retained archaic elements, as

is often true of real places. Hardbottle and Nobottle contain an element from Old English *botl,* related to *build.* Tolkien tells us that there is a town named Nobottle in Northumberland. In fact, many of his place names and hobbit surnames are used in England.

In Bree, a much older dwelling place of hobbits than the Shire, the places are represented by the oldest language of place names in the British Isles, Celtic. *Bree* (hill), *Chet* (woods), and *Combe* are to be found, the last meaning a small, deep valley, essentially the same word as *Coomb* in Rohan, and the Welsh *cwm,* a word beloved of mountaineers and creators of crossword puzzles.

Most of the oldest words among the hobbits came from a human language of Wilderland, particularly the Anduin Valley. Since the Éothéod, the ancestors of the Rohirrim, lived there at the time of the ancestors of the hobbits, their languages are related. This can be seen in words discussed in Appendix F to *The Lord of the Rings.* The hobbits' own name for themselves, *kuduk,* seems to be related to the Rohirrim's compound, *kûd-dûkan* 'hole-dweller'. To establish the relationship between the languages of the hobbits and the Rohirrim, as well as that between the Rohirrim and the Edain (men akin to them in ancient times, who migrated to Beleriand and whose language became the Westron Common Speech), the language of Rohan has been "translated" into Old English.

Again, Tolkien's explanation was probably made after the fact of giving the Rohirrim the Old English tongue. However, having done so, Tolkien had the opportunity to indulge in a lot of word-play. The Rohirrim's *kûd-dûkan* translates to Old English *hol-bytla* 'hole-builder', which could conceivably be worn down to form 'hobbit'.

One of Tolkien's most ambitious uses of Old English

was the formation of the hobbit calendar, which consists of Old English month-names changed as they might have been if English speakers had not adopted the Latin system of month-names. The hobbit month-name suffix, *-math,* is derived from the Old English *monath* 'month', as can be seen in the following list.

Hobbit Month-Names

AFTERYULE: from *aeftergeola* 'January'; *Frery* in Bree and the East-farthing from *freorig* 'freezing cold'.

SOLMATH: from *solmonath* 'February'; *sol* may mean 'mire'.

RETHE: from *réthe* 'savage', 'cruel', 'fierce' (March).

ASTRON: from *Easter-monath* 'April'; *Chithing* in Bree and the East-farthing from *cith* 'a sprout'.

THRIMIDGE: from *thri-milce* 'May'.

FORELITHE (*Lithe,* in Bree): from *lith,* the Old English word for the months of June and July.

AFTERLITHE: from *aefter-lith* 'July'; *Mede* in Bree from *med* 'middle'.

WEDMATH: from *weth* 'mild', 'gentle' (August).

HALIMATH: from *halig-monath* 'September', 'holy-month', 'month of heathen sacrifice'; called *Harvest-math* in Bree.

WINTERFILTH: from *winter-fylleth* 'October'; *Wintring* in Bree.

BLOTMATH: from *blotmonath* 'November', 'month of heathen sacrifice'; *Blooting* in Bree.

FOREYULE (*Yulemath,* in Bree and the East-farthing): from *geóla* 'December' related to the word *wheel* since at the solstice the year can be thought to have completed its circle.

Hobbit Names and Words

Andwise (OE [Old English] *and-wís* 'expert', 'skillful') A hobbit.

Anson (OE *án, sunu* 'only son') This hobbit was an only son.

Bilbo (archaic 'a slender sword or rapier known for its temper', from Bilbao, Spain, famous for its steel) Bilbo Baggins had a magic sword.

Bolger A variation on 'bulge'. Bolgers, like most hobbits, were pudgy.

Bree (archaic 'bank', 'hill') A town on a hill east of the Shire.

Brock (OE *broc* 'badger') This occurs in the hobbit surname *Brockhouse* and in Bombadil's compound, 'badger-brock'.

Budgeford A variation on 'bulge' in a ford and village in the Shire, folkland of the bulgy Bolgers.

Carl (OE, ME [Middle English] 'churl' from the Scandinavian *karl* 'man') The name of some hobbits.

Combe (Celtic 'a narrow valley or deep hollow') A village in Breeland.

Dwaling (OE *dwelian* 'to go astray', 'to wander') A village in the Shire so far afield as to be off the map to the north on a winding road.

Elfstan Fairbairn (archaic 'elfstone fairchild') A hobbit surnamed for the fair hair and faces common in the descendants of Samwise and Rose, and named for Aragorn Elessar 'Elfstone'. Elphinstone and Elbenstein are names of noble families. In folklore, old stone arrowheads found in fields were called elfstones because they were believed to have been shot at cattle by fairies to cause disease.

Fallohides Variation on fallow hide 'pale yellow pelt'. The most adventurous tribe of hobbits, so called for their fair hair.

Frodo (OE *fród* 'wise', 'prudent', 'sage', *freoda* 'protector', 'defender', *freodo* 'peace', 'security') A hobbit, the Ringbearer, and Samwise's first son. The version Froda appears in *Beowulf.*

Halfast (OE 'snug in a hall or nook') A hobbit.

Halfred (OE 'half-counselled') The name of several hobbits.

Hamfast (OE 'stay-at-home') The name of several hobbits.

Hamson (OE 'home son') A hobbit.

Harfoots (dialect 'hairfeet') The most representative tribe of hobbits.

Haysend (dialect 'hedge's end' from ME *haie* 'hedge', not 'hay, dried grass') A village in Buckland at the end of the High Hay.

Holfast (OE 'snug in hole') A hobbit.

Holman (OE 'hole man') The name of several hobbits.

Marish (dialect 'marsh') A marshy district of the Shire near the Brandywine River.

mathom (OE *mathum* 'a precious or valuable thing, often a gift') In the Shire, a gift for which the use may have been forgotten, but which one does not wish to discard.

Michel Delving (ME 'great digging') A major town in the Shire.

Samwise Gamgee (OE *sam, wís* 'half wise') A hobbit of the Fellowship of the Ring. The pun between Gamgee and Cotton implied on the last page of the appendices involves Gamgee bandage, consisting of gauze over cotton wool, named for the surgeon who invented it.

Scary (dialect *scar* 'rocky cliff' related to *skerry* 'a low rock in the sea') A village in the Shire.

Smial (OE *smygel* 'a burrow', 'place to creep into') A hobbit hole.

Staddle (dialect 'the foundation of a building, barn, or shed') A village in Breeland.

Stoor (dialect *stour* 'numerous', 'bulky', 'stout', 'sturdy', 'stubborn') The tribe of hobbits that were stoutest and heaviest in build.

Thain (OE *thegn* 'a member of one of several ranks between earls and freemen') A hereditary title of leadership among the Tooks.

Withywindle (dialect *withywind* 'bindweed') The Withywindle River followed a winding course and snared travelers.

The Language
of the Rohirrim

The language of the Rohirrim reflects the history of their migrations and of the peoples with whom they were in contact and whose language they in turn influenced.

The Rohirrim had, at the time of the War of the Rings, only lived in Rohan for some five hundred years. Their origins, as far as they are known, were in the middle Anduin Valley. It was here that they may have met the hobbit ancestors. Smeagol's people, related to the Stoors who remained in or returned to Wilderland, lived in that region.

The ancestors of the Rohirrim migrated north to the upper Anduin Valley, led by Frumgar, as Mirkwood became an evil place. They took the name *Éothéod* 'Horsefolk', which they also gave to their new land. However, they remained friendly with the other free peoples on the Anduin. When the Steward of Gondor sent to them for aid against an invasion of Orcs and Easterlings, Eorl, leader of the Éothéod, brought south a cavalry of knights who were decisive in the victory of the battle of the Field of Celebrant. Gratefully, the Steward Cirion gave them Calenardhon, 'The Green Region' of northern Gondor, for their own land. The men of Gondor called the Éothéod the *Rohirrim* 'Masters of Horses' in the Gray-Elven tongue, and called their land *Rohan,* 'Horse Country', in the same language.

Most names in Rohan were appropriate to the people who bore them. Rulers often had names meaning prince, earl, lord, or chief. *Wormtongue* was an actual Old English compound word for a sarcastic person. The *orm* in the original form means 'serpent', not the garden variety of worm. Many other names refer to the horses so essential to the Rohirrim's way of life. Plainly, this process of naming indicates that the Rohirrim, like such peoples as the American Indians, were given names in adulthood that reflected their attributes.

All of the words and names of the Rohirrim used in the text of *The Lord of the Rings* are Old English or archaic English translations, just as the Westron language in the text is entirely translated into English.

Words and Names in Rohan

Aldor (OE 'an elder', 'chief') A king of Rohan who lived to a great age.

Anborn (OE *án-boren* 'only-born', 'only-begotten') A Ranger of Ithilien.

Arod (OE 'quick', 'swift', 'ready') The horse Legolas and Gimli rode in Rohan.

athelas (OE *athel* 'noble' with a plural suffix, forming the Elvish element, *las* 'leaf') Aragorn's healing herb.

Baldor (OE 'more bold, courageous, honorable, hence a

prince, ruler') This bold son of a king of Rohan went into the Paths of the Dead and was lost.

Béma (OE *bema* or *beme* 'trumpet') The name in Rohan for the Vala Oromë. *Oromë* means 'Sound of Horns', 'Hornblowing' in Elvish.

Brytta (OE 'bestower, dispenser, distributor, hence a prince, lord') A very generous king of Rohan.

Ceorl (OE 'a freeman of the lowest class', 'churl', 'husbandman') A rider of Rohan.

Coomb (Celtic 'narrow valley or deep hollow') Deeping Coomb was the valley below Hornburg.

Déor (OE 'deer', 'wild animal', 'brave or bold as a wild beast') A king of Rohan.

Deorwine (OE 'deer-friend', 'friend of wild animals') A rider of Rohan.

Derndingle (OE *dern* 'secret', ME *dingle* 'dell') The hollow where Entmoots were held.

Dernhelm (OE 'secret helmet', 'helmet of secrecy') The name Éowyn took when she rode to Gondor disguised in man's armor.

Dunharg, Dunharrow (OE *dún hearg* 'hill temple') A secret temple in Rohan built by a forgotten people, probably ancestors of the Dead.

Dúnhere (OE 'hill warrior') A rider of Rohan.

Dunland, Dunlending (OE *dún-land* 'hill-land', 'down-land' in contrast to OE *feld-land* 'plain-land', 'level-land') Since Dunland with this meaning is an actual OE compound word, Tolkien makes a scholarly pun when he derives Dunland from OE *dunn* 'dark brown', because of the swarthy coloring of the Dunlendings, the wild inhabitants of the lands west of Rohan.

Dwimmerlaik (ME *dweomerlaik* 'legerdemain' from OE *dwimor* 'illusion') Éowyn belittled the Captain of the

Nazgûl by calling him a trick of Sauron's magic.

Dwimorberg (OE 'haunted mountain', 'mountain of phantoms') The mountain under which lay the Paths of the Dead.

Dwimordene (OE 'valley of illusion') The name in Rohan for Lothlórien.

Eastemnet (OE 'east plain') The lands of Rohan east of the Entwash.

Eastfold (OE 'east earth') An eastern division of Rohan.

Edoras (OE 'dwellings', 'places enclosed by a barrier') The palisaded royal city of Rohan.

Elfhelm (OE 'elf helmet') A rider of Rohan.

Elfwine (OE 'elf-friend') A king of Rohan, son of Éomer.

Ent (OE 'giant') The name in Rohan for the tree-giants in Fangorn Forest. This word for giant appears in *Beowulf.*

Éomer (OE 'horse mare') A hero and king of Rohan. This name appears in *Beowulf.*

Éomund (OE 'horse hand') A rider of Rohan.

Éored (OE 'cavalry') A cavalry unit of the Rohirrim.

Eorl (OE 'a nobleman of high rank', 'an earl') The first king of Rohan.

Éothain (OE 'horse thane' from *thegn* 'thane, a member of any of several classes between earls and freemen') A rider of Rohan.

Éothéod (OE 'horse folk') The ancestors of the Rohirrim and their land in the upper Anduin Valley.

Éowyn (OE 'one who delights in horses') A renowned woman of Rohan.

Erkenbrand (OE 'chief torch') A rider of Rohan.

Fastred (OE 'firm counsel') A king of Rohan's son.

Felaróf (OE 'very valiant', 'strong') Eorl's horse.

Fengel (OE 'prince') A king of Rohan.

Firienfeld, Firienwood (OE 'mountain field', 'mountain

wood' from *firgen* 'mountain') The field of Dunharrow and a forest at the foot of the White Mountains.

Folca (OE *folc* 'folk', 'people') A king of Rohan.

Folcred (OE 'counsellor of the people') A king of Rohan's son.

Folcwine (OE 'friend of the people') A king of Rohan.

Folde (OE *fold* 'the earth') A division of Rohan.

Fram (OE 'firm', 'valiant', 'stout') A lord of Éothéod.

Fréa (OE 'lord', 'master') A king of Rohan.

Fréaláf (OE 'survivor of lords') A king of Rohan, who, as Helm's nephew, became his heir when Helm and his sons died during the Long Winter.

Fréawine (OE 'dear or beloved lord') A king of Rohan.

Freca (OE 'a bold man', 'warrior or hero', from *frec* 'greedy', 'audacious') A greedy, proud man of Rohan who set himself up as Helm's rival.

Frumgar (OE 'first spear') The first lord of the Éothéod.

Galmod (OE 'light, wanton mood') The father of Grima Wormtongue.

Gamling (OE 'old one' from *gamol* 'old', 'aged') An old man at Helm's Deep.

Garulf (OE 'spear wolf') A rider of Rohan.

Gleowine (OE 'friend of minstrelsy') Théoden's minstrel.

Goldwine (OE 'gold friend') A king of Rohan.

Grima Wormtongue (OE *grim* 'grim', 'fierce', 'cruel', 'a mask', 'a specter') *Wormtongue* was an actual OE compound word used to describe sarcastic or bitter-spoken people. Théoden's traitorous counsellor.

Guthlaf (OE 'surviver of battle') Théoden's standard-bearer, who, in spite of his name, died in the Battle of Pelennor Field.

Guthwine (OE 'battle-friend') A common OE kenning for swords. Éomer's sword.

Haleth (OE 'more hale') Helm's son.

Halifirien (OE *halig, firgen* 'holy mountain') A beacon hill in Firienwood.

Háma (OE 'a coat of mail') The name of Helm's youngest son and of Théoden's doorward.

Harding (OE *hearding* 'a brave man', 'warrior', 'hero') A rider of Rohan.

Hasufel (OE 'gray coat'. *hasu* 'gray', 'tawney', 'ash-colored') Aragorn's horse in Rohan.

Helm (OE 'helmet') A king of Rohan.

Herefara (OE 'war farer') A rider of Rohan.

Herubrand (OE 'war torch') A rider of Rohan.

Herugrim (OE 'fierce in war') Theoden's sword.

Hild (OE 'battle') This was the name of a Valkyrie, and so was considered appropriate as a name for women. Helm's sister.

Holdwine (OE 'true friend') The name Éomer gave Meriadoc. The punning implications of this name are obvious.

Horn (OE 'horn') A rider of Rohan.

Irensaga (OE 'iron saw') A saw-toothed mountain near Dunharrow.

Isen River (OE 'iron') The river forming the western boundary of Rohan.

Isengard (OE 'iron yard'. *geard* 'enclosure') Saruman's fortress in a circle of hills.

Láthspell (OE 'evil news') The name Wormtongue called Gandalf.

Léod (OE 'man', 'one of a people or country') A lord of Éotheod, the father of Eorl.

Léofa (OE *leof* 'loved', 'dear') The name given to Brytta, a very generous king of Rohan.

Mark (OE *mearc* 'territory within a boundary') This element is seen in the word *Denmark.* The country of Rohan.

Mearas (OE 'horses') The horses of the kings of Rohan.

Meduseld (OE 'mead-hall') The standard OE word for a hall where feasting took place. The royal hall of Rohan.

Mering Stream (dialect 'fixing a boundary') The stream forming an eastern border of Rohan.

Mundburg, Mundberg OE *mund-beorg* is an actual OE compound word meaning 'sheltering hill' and appears in the text in the form *Mundburg.* The index gives the form *Mundberg* and the translation 'sheltering fortress'. Probably both the fortress of Minas Tirith and the hill upon which it stood were referred to in these names given them by the Rohirrim.

Orc (OE 'demon' from Latin *Orcus,* the god of the Dead) A member of the evil goblin tribes. The word appears in *Beowulf.*

Orthanc (OE 'intelligence', 'skill', 'mechanical art') In Sindarin Elvish 'mount fang', 'fang fort'. Saruman's tower in Isengard.

Púkel-men OE *púcel, puckle* 'a demon, goblin, or wood-wose' related to the Irish *púca* 'sprite' and to Shakespeare's Puck. *Puckle* is a word still used in dialect English for an ugly, misshapen person. Sculptures on the road to Dunharrow resembling Woses.

Sauruman (OE 'crafty man'. *searu* 'craft', 'device', 'wile') The word can be used either in a good or a bad sense. A wizard.

simbelmyne (OE 'ever mind') White flowers that grew in Rohan on the barrows of the dead kings.

Stybba (OE *stybb* 'stub', 'stump') The pony that Meriadoc rode in Rohan.

Thengel (OE 'a prince') A king of Rohan.

Théoden (OE 'chief of a nation or a people') A king of Rohan.

Théodred (OE 'people's counsel') The son of King Théoden.

Théodwyn (OE 'delight of the people') A woman of Rohan.

Thrihyrne (OE 'three horn') The mountain above Helm's Deep.

Walda (OE *weald* 'powerful', 'mighty') A king of Rohan.

Westemnet (OE 'west plain') The western lands of Rohan.

Wetwang (dialect 'wet country'. *wang* 'field, country, place') The marshes at the meeting of the Entwash and the Anduin.

Widfara (OE 'wide farer') A rider of Rohan.

Wight (OE *wiht* 'a creature', 'a thing', 'a whit') A spirit or specter haunting barrows.

Windfola (OE 'wind foal') The horse that Éowyn and Meriadoc rode to Minas Tirith.

Wold (OE 'open, hilly district') A part of Rohan.

Woses (ME *woodwose* OE *wuduwasa* 'a satyr-like woods-demon') Tolkien translates *wasa* as 'forlorn, abandoned person' and suggests that *wuduwasa* first referred to actual people who had taken to the woods for survival. A forest-dwelling, tribal people in the White Mountains. Woodwoses are mentioned in *Sir Gawain and the Green Knight.*

Wulf (OE 'wolf') A man who temporarily usurped the throne of Rohan.

The Languages
of Rhovannion

In Rhovannion, Wilderland, near the place of origin of both the hobbits and the Rohirrim, many peoples were isolated by the great expanses of the forest later known as Mirkwood, where they developed various languages of their own. These people, like the ancient horselords, were related to the Edain who migrated to Beleriand and whose language became the Common Speech.

The rulers of the horselords claimed kinship with the kings of Rhovannion. One king of Rhovannion's daughter wedded Eldacar, King of Gondor, thus something was recorded about the woodland kings. Vidugavia has the name of a Gothic smith-god, recorded by Jacob Grimm as *Vidugauja,* that is, differing from Tolkien's spelling only in the letters interchangeable in medieval writing, *u–v* and *j–i.* The first element of the name, *vidus,* Gothic for 'forest', also appears in the name of Vidugavia's daughter, Vidumavi.

The rest of the peoples' languages are represented by

either Old English or Scandinavian languages. The latter is most evident in *The Hobbit,* in which Smaug, wargs, and Mirkwood itself have northern origins. Where Scandinavian languages are used, they indicate a further linguistic departure from Westron than that represented by Old English.

The Dwarves, who were supposed to have taken their use-names from the language of the men around them, have the names of Dwarves in the Icelandic *Prose Edda.* These names often rhyme or are alliterative. Strangely, many of the Dwarf names for which there are translations refer to the dead. The Teutonic peoples associated Dwarves with the spirits of the dead, possibly because of their underground dwellings. It is interesting to note that *nain,* the modern French word for Dwarf, is a Dwarf name occurring both in Tolkien's works and in the *Prose Edda.*

The tradition that Dwarves' names in their own language were secret may have begun when Tolkien, who had already established a Dwarf language in *The Silmarillion,* departed from it in *The Hobbit* and later had to explain the discrepancy. At least one Dwarf in *The Silmarillion* has his Dwarvish name given: Azaghâl, Lord of Belegost. Perhaps Dwarves were less secretive then, or perhaps Azaghâl is a title, not a name.

Words and Names in Rhovannion

Arkenstone (OE *eorcan-stán* 'genuine', 'holy stone') The glowing jewel, heart of the Lonely Mountain.

Bard (OE) This is hypothesized to be the original form of the word 'beard'. In Celtic, *bard* means poet. Bard was the man of Laketown who killed the dragon Smaug.

Beorn (OE 'man', 'hero' Scandinavian *bjorn* 'bear') A

clever name for the man of Wilderland who could turn himself into a bear.

Brand (OE 'firebrand', 'torch') A king of Dale descended from Bard.

Carrock (northern dialect 'stone', 'rock' from OE *carr* 'stone', 'rock') Compare with the Scottish *cairn* 'a marker or monument built of piled stones'. The stone island in the upper Anduin River named by Beorn.

Dain (Old Norse *Dáinn* 'corpse') The name of two kings of the Dwarves.

Déagol (OE 'secret', 'unknown') Gollum's friend, the finder of the One Ring. An unconfirmed source indicates that Sméagol and Déagol were Old English titles for Cain and Abel.

Durin (Old Norse *Durinn,* in Scandinavian mythology, one of two mysterious princes who formed new Dwarves out of earth) An ancestor of the Dwarves.

Dwalin (Old Norse *Dvalinn* 'one lying in a trance') A Dwarf of Thorin's company.

Dwerrowdelf Tolkien's invented form of *Dwarf-delving. Dwerrow* is a hypothetical word showing how OE *dweorg* 'dwarf' might have evolved to parallel such words as OE *beorg* 'barrow'. The translation of **Phurunargian,** the Westron name of **Khazad-dûm,** Moria.

Forn (Scandinavian 'ancient', 'sorcery') The Dwarvish name of Bombadil.

Fundin (Old Norse 'found one') A Dwarf, the father of Balin and Dwalin.

Gandalf (Old Norse *Ganndálf* 'sorcerer elf') A wizard.

Gimli (Old Norse 'lee of flame', 'highest heaven') A Dwarf, one of the fellowship of the ring.

Incánus (Latin 'quite gray') The name given to Gandalf in the south.

Náin (Old Norse *Nainn* 'corpse') The name of three Dwarves, two of them kings.

Nár (Old Norse 'corpse') A Dwarf.

Oin (Old Norse 'fearful') A Dwarf of Thorin's company.

Olorin (Old High German *Alarûn,* Old Norse *Olrun* 'a prophetic and diabolic spirit', 'a mandrake root') Gandalf's name in the West in his youth.

Orald (OE 'very old' or 'original', 'early') Bombadil's name among men.

Ori (Old Norse 'raging one') A Dwarf in Thorin's company.

Radagast (Slavonic *Radegast, Radihost* from *rad* 'glad', *radost* 'joy') The Slavonic god of bliss, good counsel, and honor, associated with the Roman god Mercury and the Greek god Hermes, traditional god of wizards. A wizard from Wilderland.

Scatha (OE 'malefactor', compare 'scathe') A dragon.

Shelob (ME 'she spider' *lob* and *cob* are both from OE *coppe* 'spider' originally meaning 'pendulous'. *Attercop* means 'poison spider', compare 'adder') A giant she-spider.

Smaug (Norwegian, a form of *smyge* 'slip', 'sneak', 'steal') A dragon. **Smaug, Sméagol,** and **Smial** are related words.

Sméagol (OE *smeah* 'penetrating', 'creeping') Gollum.

Thorin Oakenshield (Old Norse *Thorin* 'bold one', *Eikenskjaldi* 'with oak shield' the names of two different Dwarves in the *Prose Edda*) A Dwarf-lord.

Thráin (Old Norse *Thráinn* 'obstinate') The name of two kings of the Dwarves.

Tindrock (OE 'tine rock', *tind* 'tine', 'spine', 'tooth of a fork') An island above Rauros.

Variags (Slavonic *Varyags* was a name for Scandinavian

warriors) Allies of Sauron from Khand in the east.

Vidugavia (Gothic *Vidugáuja,* a smith-god of the type of the English god Weland, from Gothic *vidus* 'forest') A king of Rhovannion, the land in and around Mirkwood.

Warg (Scandinavian *varg* 'wolf') Evil wolves that hunted with the Orcs.

Quotations Translated

Following are quotations in the languages of Middle-earth from *The Silmarillion, The Lord of the Rings,* and Humphrey Carpenter's authorized biography, *Tolkien.* Translations by Tolkien are in quotation marks, my hypothesized translations are in parentheses. The hymn to Galadriel from Rivendell, Galadriel's lament, and Samwise's prayer are given in Tolkien's literal translation from *The Road Goes Ever On.* The quotations, which include all those available in Tolkien's invented languages, are given in chronological order.

*

Part of a poem dated November 1916, March 1916. Quenya, T/76.

> *Ai lintulinda Lasselanta*
> (O swiftly sing of autumn
> *Pilingeve suyer nalla ganta*
> cry

Kuluvi ya karnevalinar
Red-gold-will which red fire of power
V'ematte singi Eldamar.
            Elvenhome.)

Fingon's cry at the Nirnaeth Arnoediad. Quenya, S/190.

Utúlie'n aurë! Aiya Eldalie ar
"The day has come! Behold, people of the Eldar and
Atanatári, utúlie'n auré!
Fathers of Men, the day has come!"

The response of those who heard Fingon. Quenya, S/190.

Auta i lómë!
"The night is passing!"

The cry of Hurin as he fought to the last at the Nirnaeth
Arnoediad. Quenya, S/195.

Aurë entuluva!
"Day shall come again!"

Nienor's farewell to Turin. Quenya, S/223.

A Túrin Turambar turun ambartanen.
"Master of doom by doom mastered."

Frodo's greeting to Gildor in the Shire. Quenya, 1/90.

Elen síla lumenn' omentielvo.
"A star shines on the hour of our meeting."

Glorfindel's greeting to Strider on the road to the Ford of
Rivendell. Sindarin, 1/222.

Ai na vedui Dúnadan! Mae govannen!
(O, [it] is [at] last Dúnadan!)

Glorfindel's cry to his horse as Frodo rides. Sindarin,
1/225.

Noro lim, noro lim, Asfaloth!
"Ride on, ride on, Asfaloth!"

The hymn to Elbereth sung in Elrond's house. Sindarin, 1/250.

A Elbereth   Gilthoniel
"O Star-Queen, Star-Kindler
silivren   penna   míriel
(white) glittering slants down sparkling like jewels
o   menel   aglar   elenath!
from firmament glory (of the) star-host!
Na-chaered palan-díriel
To-remote distance after having gazed
o   galadhremmin ennorath
from treewoven   middle-earth,
Fanuilos   le   linnathon
Snow-white, to thee I will chant
nef   aear, si nef   aearon!
on this side of the ocean, here on this side of the great ocean!"

The inscription on the One Ring, recited by Gandalf at the Council of Elrond. Black Speech, 1/267.

Ash nazg durbatulûk,
"One Ring to rule them all,
Ash nazg gimbatul,
One Ring to find them,
Ash nazg thrakatulûk,
One Ring to bring them all
Agh burzum-ishi krimpatul.
and in the Darkness bind them."

Gandalf's spell producing fire on Caradhras. Sindarin, 1/304.

Naur an edraith ammen!
(Fire . . .)

Gandalf's spell producing fire against the wolves below Caradhras. Sindarin, 1/312.

> *Naur an edraith ammen!*
> (Fire . . .
> *Naur dan i ngaurhoth!*
> Fire take the werewolves!)

The inscription over the west gate of Moria. Sindarin, 1/319.

> *Ennyn   Durin Aran   Moria:*
> "The doors of Durin Lord of Moria:
> *pedo   mellon a   minno.*
> speak friend and enter.
> *Im Narvi hain echant:*
> I, Narvi made them:
> *Celebrimbor o Eregion teithant i thiw hin.*
> Celebrimbor of Hollin drew these signs."

Gandalf's spell to open the Moria gate. Sindarin, 1/320.

> *Annon edhellen,   edro hi ammen!*
> (Door of the elves open . . .
> *Fennas   Nogothrim, lasto   beth   lammen!*
> Gateway of Dwarf-folk, listen to the word of my voice.)

Aragorn's farewell to Arwen from Lórien. Quenya, 1/367.

> *Arwen vanimelda, namarië!*
> (Arwen, fair-love, farewell!)

Altariello naine Lóriendesse: Galadriel's lament in Lorien. Quenya, 1/394.

> *"Ai!   laurië   lantar   lassi súrinen,*
> "Alas! golden [pl.] fall [pl.] leaves wind-in,
> *Yéni   ú-nót-imë   ve rámar aldaron!*
> Years not-count-able as wings trees-of!

Yéni   ve   lintë   yuldar   avánier
Years like swift [pl.] draughts have passed away [pl.]
mi   oro-mardi   lisse-miruvóre-va
in the high-halls sweet-nectar-of
Andúnë pella   Vardo   tellumar
west   beyond (the borders of), Varda's domes
nu   luini yassen   tintilar i eleni
under blue   which-in [pl.] twinkle the stars
óma-ryo   aire-tári-lírinen.
voice-hers holy-queen-song-in.
Sí   man   i   yulma nin   en-quant-uva?
Now who the cup   me-for re-fill-will?
An   sí   Tintallë   Varda Oio-lossëo
For now Star-Kindler Varda Ever-white-from
ve   fanyar má-rya-t   Elen-tári   ortanë
like (white) clouds hands-her-two Star-Queen lifted-up
ar   ilyë   tier   undu-lávë   lumbulë;
and all [pl.] roads down-licked (heavy) shadow;
ar   sinda-nórie-llo   caita mornië
and gray-country-from lies   darkness
i   falma-li-nnar   imbë   met,   ar hísië
the foaming-waves-many-upon [pl.] between us-two, and mist
un-túpa   Calaciryo   míri   oialë.
down-roofs Calacirya's jewels everlastingly.
Sí   vanwa ná   Rómello   vanwa,   Valimar!
Now lost is, (to one) from the East lost, Valimar!
Namárië!   Nai   hir-uva-lyë   Valimar.
Farewell!   Be it that find-wilt-thou Valimar.
Nai   elyë   hir-uva.   Namárië!
Be it that even-thou find-will (it). Farewell!"

A Mordor-Orc's curse on the Orcs of Saruman. Debased
Black Speech, 2/48.

Uglúk u bagronk sha pushdug Saruman-glob búbhosh skai.
(Untranslatable.)

Treebeard's description of Lórien. Quenya, 2/70.

> *Laurelindórenan   lindelorendor   malinorélion   orn-*
> *emalin.*
> (Golden-song-land-vale song-gold-land gold-tree-beech tree-
> golden.)

Treebeard's description of Fangorn Forest. Quenya, 2/70.

> *Taurelilómëa-tumbalemorna   Tumbaletaurëa*
> "Forest-many-shadowed deep-valley-black deep-valley-for-
> ested
> *Lómëanor.*
> Gloomyland."

Frodo's praise of the light of Galadriel in Shelob's lair.
Quenya 2/329.

> *Aiya   Earendil Elenion   Ancalima!*
> (Behold Eärendil Star [of] Long-Light!)

Samwise's call to Elbereth as he attacks Shelob. Sindarin,
2/339.

> *A Elbereth   Gilthoniel*
> "O Star-Queen Star-Kindler
> *o   menel   palan-díriel,*
> from firmament afar-gazing,
> *le   nallon sí di'nguruthos!*
> to thee I cry here beneath death-horror!
> *A tíro   nin,   Fanuilos!*
> O watch over me, Fanuilos!"

The people praise the Halflings on the Field of Cormallen.
Sindarin, 3/231.

> *Cuio i Pheriain anann! Aglar'ni   Pheriannath!*
> (Live the Halflings long!   Glorify the Halflings!

> *Daur a Berhael, Conin en   Annûn! Eglerio!*
>   . . . of the West!   Glorify them!
> *Eglerio!*
> Glorify them!
> *A laita te, laita te! Andave laituvalmet!*
> O praise them, praise them!   praise-will-we!
> *Cormacolindor, a laita tárienna!*
> Ringbearers,   o praise . . .)

Elessar's coronation oath, the words spoken by Elendil upon his landing in Middle-earth. Quenya, 3/245.

> *Et Eärello   Endorenna   utúlien.*
> "Out of the Great Sea to Middle-earth I am come.
> *Sinome   maruvan   ar   Hildinyar*
> In this place will I abide, and my heirs,
> *tenn'   Ambar-metta!*
> unto the ending of the world!"

Elessar's exclamation upon finding the sapling of the White Tree. Quenya, 3/250.

> *Yé!   utúvienyes!*
> "I have found it!"

Treebeard's farewell to Galadriel. Quenya, 3/259.

> *A   vanimar,   vanimálion nostari!*
> (O   fair-home, fair-gold . . . queen!)

The despairing *linnod* of Gilraen, Aragorn's mother. Sindarin, 3/342.

> *Onen i-Estel Edain,   ú-chebin estel anim.*
> "I gave Hope to the Dunedain, I have kept no hope for myself."

Runes and Letters

Anglo-Saxon Runes

ᚣ	F	ᚺ	H	ᛗ	E
ᚻ	U/V	✛	N	ᛈ	M
ᚦ	TH	ᛁ	I	ᚱ	L
ᚬ	O	ᚭ	J	ᚷ	NG
ᚱ	R	ᛈ	P	⊠	D
ᚺ	K	ᛉ	Z	ᛤ	D
ᛁ	C	ᚺ	S	ᚱ	A
ᚷ	G	↑	T	ᚯ	EE/OE
ᛈ	W	ᛒ	B	ᚻ	Y

The runes in the adjacent chart are those shown on the map in *The Hobbit.* They are one of several types actually used by writers of Old English and other Germanic languages. They are listed in their original Old English order, the first six letters of which give runes their alternate name, *futhork.*

The dedication to this book is written in this runic alphabet, using the standard punctuation, four dots in a vertical line before or after sentences, two dots in a colon between words. These symbols can be used for English, Germanic languages, or Tolkien's languages.

Cirth or Angerthas

Tolkien used the Anglo-Saxon runic symbols and variations, reversals, and inversions for the alphabets called Cirth or Angerthas, meaning runes, or, more literally, "engraved" letters. The forms of Tolkien's adapted runes signify linguistic sound relationships. An extra stroke is added to the voiced sound where there are pairs of voiced and unvoiced sounds. In general, the Cirth numbered 1 through 28 represent sounds that are articulated progressively from the front to the back of the mouth. Numbers 29 through 33 are liquid sounds with no specific point of articulation. The vowels 39 through 45 are sounded in the top of the mouth from front to back, 46 through 52 are sounded in the bottom of the mouth from front to back. The rest of the Cirth are miscellaneous symbols.

The Cirth shown below were used primarily for incised inscriptions. When separated by –, those on the left are the older *Angerthas,* those on the right are the values of the Dwarvish *Angerthas Moria,* those marked with ** are the values used by the Dwarves of Erebor, as in the Book of Mazarbul, and the values in parentheses () were those used by the Elves. Cirth marked * were used by Dwarves only.

1	ⴘ p		16	zh**
2	b		17	nj – z – ks**
3	f		18	k
4	v		19	g
5	hw		20	kh
6	m		21	gh
7	(mh) mb		22	ng – n
8	t		23	kw
9	d		24	gw
10	th		25	khw
11	dh		26	ghw – w
12	n – r		27	ngw
13	ch		28	nw
14	j**		29	r – j – g**
15	sh		30	rh – zh –gh**

31	⺅	l	46	H	e
32	⻌	lh	47	⻌	ē
33	⽊	ng — nd	48	⼓	a
34	⼃	s — h	49	⼓	ā
35	⼁	s — '	50	⼈	o
36	⼃	z — ng	51	⼌⼌	ō
37	⼃	ng*	52	⼈⼈	ö
38	⼌ ⼌	nd — nj	53	⼁	n*
39	⼁	i (y)	54	⼈	h — s
40	⼓	y*	55	⼁⼁	ə*
41	N	hy*	56	⼁⼁	ə*
42	⼓	u	57	⼁	ps**
43	⼓	ū — z**	58	⼃	ts**
44	⼓	w		⼁	+h
45	⼓⼓	ü	&	⼌	&

Tengwar

p	t	*tinco*	'metal'
pɔ	d/nd*	*ando*	'gate'
b	th	*thule, sule*	'spirit'
bɔ	dh nt*	*anto*	'mouth'
ɱɔ	n	*numen*	'west'
ɳ	r	*ore*	'heart'
ɣ	r	*romen*	'east'
ʗ	s	*silme*	'starlight'
λ	h	*hyarmen*	'south'

The Feanorean Tengwar or Tiw 'letters' shown above and on the following three pages were used for writing with brush or pen. The values marked * were only used in Quenya. The values marked ? are hypothetically reconstructed from their names.

p	p	*parma*	'book'
p	b/mb*	*umbar*	'fate'
b	f	*formen*	'north'
b	v mp*	*ampa*	'hook'
m	m	*malta*	'gold'
n	w/v*	*vala*	'angelic power'
y	rh rd*	*arda*	'region'
ʔ	s	*silme nuquerna*	's reversed'
d	hw	*hwesta sindarinwa*	'Gray-Elven hw'

ᴄʃ	c/k	*calma*	'lamp'
ᴄᴄʃ	j/g ng*	*anga*	'iron'
ᴅ	sh/hk	*harma, aha*	'treasure, rage'
ᴄᴅ	zh/gh nk*	*anca*	'jaws'
ᴄᴄʃ	n/ng?	*noldo, ngoldo*	'one of the Noldor'
ᴄᴜ	y	*anna*	'gift'
ᴦ	l	*lambe*	'tongue'
ε	z	*áre, áze, esse*	'sunlight, name'
λ	y	*yanta*	'bridge'

Ϥ k/kw *quesse*
        'feather'

ᡈᏁ g/gw *ungwe*
   ngw* 'spider's web'

ᡑ ch/khw *hwesta*
   hw   'breeze'

ᡐᏁ gh/ghw *unque*
   w/nqu* 'a hollow'

ᡒᏁ ngw? *nwalme, ngwalme*
          'torment'

ᡒ w?   *vilya, wilya*
         'air, sky'

Ϩ lh/ld* *alda*
          'tree'

Ȝ z   *áre nuquerna*
         'z reversed'

ᴑ w   *ure*
         'heat'

Tehtar (vowel signs)

∴ or ∧	A
╱ or •	E
• or ╱	I
↱ or ꝯ	O
ꝯ or ↱	U

~ used over a consonant, shows that the consonant is preceded by a nasal (N or M) of the
same series: nt, mp, nk.

⟩ attached to the bow of a consonant indicates a
following S.

Vowels written as separate letters and other special con-
ventions often used in Sindarin, as in the inscription over
the west gate of Moria:

⊂ A		╱ *andaith* 'long mark' marks a vowel of
		long duration
⋏ E		
╱ I	ᴅᴅ nn	
ᴜ O	ᴅ n	
○ U	ᴅ m	
⊃ Y		

The Cirth, or Angerthas, called "runes," can be used for
writing English and Dwarvish (as on Balin's Tomb) as
well as for writing Elvish. They may have been used for
the Black Speech as well. The Tengwar, or Tîw, called
"letters," can be used to write English (as on the title pages
of *The Lord of the Rings* and *The Silmarillion*), Black
Speech (as on the One Ring), or (as Ori wrote in the Book
of Mazarbul) Dwarvish or Westron (The language is not

specified.) The Tengwar were designed by the Elves for writing the Elvish languages. The two major Elvish languages in Tolkien's works are Sindarin (Gray-Elven, as in the chant to Elbereth) and Quenya (High-Elven, as in Galadriel's Lament).

A complete guide to the use of vowels in written Tengwar, or Elvish Script, is given in Appendix E to *The Lord of the Rings,* in the note to the section on the Fëanorean letters. As explained there, the *tehtar,* or vowel marks, are written above the preceding consonant in such languages as Quenya in which words usually end with a vowel. In Sindarin, in which words usually begin with a vowel, the vowel mark is placed over the following consonant. The inscription on the west gate of Moria, in Sindarin, uses a mode in which a separate letter is used for each vowel. This mode is very convenient for the writer accustomed to an alphabet like that of English, in which vowels are separate letters. The subtitle of this book, in Quenya, is written in that "full writing" mode (the calligraphic style is individual to this author).

It is interesting to note that in early calligraphy (some examples of which appear in the Ballantine *Silmarillion Desk Calendar* for 1979), Tolkien used vowels closer in shape and value to the English vowels in writing the "full" mode of Elvish script, at least when writing in English. The west gate inscription may show a departure to a more foreign alphabet, which may have evolved to a final form in which the vowels are *tehta* superscriptions.

PART II

THE ELVISH LANGUAGES

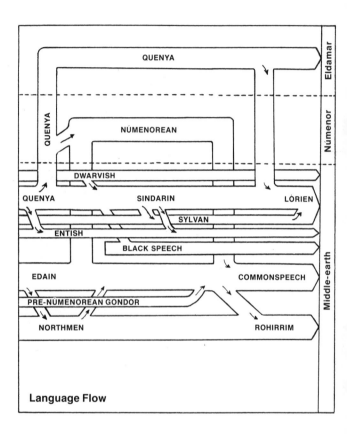

Language Flow

The Elven Tongues
and the
Power of Language

It is significant in Tolkien's works that the spoken word is essential for the Creation. It is not specified whether there are words in the song of the Ainur, but it is certain that the song was made manifest by the word of Iluvatar: *Ea!* 'Let it be!' This is comparable to the biblical account of the Creation, when the spoken word of Yahweh brought forth what was essential to the universe.

On earth the Ainur are described as speaking, having names, holding councils, and, perhaps most significantly, creating through the use of voice, as Yavanna did when she sang the song that brought forth the Two Trees.

Aulë, when he made the Dwarves, 'instructed them in the language he had devised for them' (*Silmarillion,* p. 43). Presumably they retained that language when they reawakened. One of the many unique features of the Dwarves is that their language was devised for them by a Vala, rather than evolving naturally as did the languages of men and Elves.

*

When the Elves first awoke, before they had met any of the Ainur or other speaking creatures, they called themselves the Quendi, 'those that speak with voices.' In Elvish lore it is said that the Elves awoke after Varda had kindled the nearest and brightest stars. They saw these lights in the sunless world and were strangely moved, crying, *Ele!* 'Behold!', from which exclamation came their word for the stars they revered ever afterward.

When the Vala Oromë discovered the Elves, he called them *Eldar* 'of the stars' in their own tongue. However, that name was only retained by the Elves who began the Great Journey following Oromë into the West.

Comments on the evolution and significance of language are made throughout *The Silmarillion.* The Quenya language, which is the High Elven speech, Tolkien called Eldarin, although this is not entirely accurate. The Eldar included all the Elves who at least began the journey west, although some of them remained in Beleriand and became the Sindar, the Gray-Elves who spoke Sindarin, a separate language. Tolkien more accurately called Quenya the tongue of Valinor. Whether the Ainur taught the Elves their language or only added elements to that language, the Quenya tongue, rich and expressive, developed over the long ages of the time of the Two Trees.

The Teleri, the Sea Elves, lived a long age on the island of Tol Eressea, thus their language became different from that of the other High Elves, the Vanyar and the Noldor. However, when they had moved the Alqualondë they were apparently able to understand and refuse the demands of the Noldor led by Fëanor.

The High Elves, or Caliquendi, 'Elves of Light', who had lived in the light of the Two Trees, had been separated from the Moriquendi, 'Elves of Darkness', for three ages

before the exiled Noldor returned from Eldamar to Beleriand, and in that time their languages diverged.

At the Mereth Aderthad, 'the Feast of Reuniting', held
by Fingolfin to unite the allies against the Enemy, Sindarin
was spoken, even by the Noldor, who learned it more
readily than the Gray Elves (the Sindar) could learn the
tongue of Valinor.

When Thingol, whose brother was king of the Teleri
who were slain at Alqulondë, heard of the Kinslaying, he
commanded that no Sindarin Elf should speak or answer
in Quenya, the language of the Noldor who had begun the
slaying. He vowed that any who used the Quenya tongue
in his realm would be considered unrepentant kinslayers
and betrayers of their people. The Sindar accepted the
decree. The Noldorin exiles adopted the Sindarin language for general use. Quenya, the High Speech, was only
spoken by the lords of the Noldor, but wherever the Noldor lived, they retained Quenya as a language of lore. For
this reason, Galadriel, who was high among the Noldor,
sang her lament for the West in Quenya as she watched
the Fellowship of the Ring depart from Lórien.

*

The languages of Middle-earth retained a vital power. The
right user or the right words could unleash significant
powers for good or for evil.

It was said of the Silmarils that they were "cursed with
an oath of hatred, and he that even names them in desire
moves a great power from slumber" (*Silmarillion,* p. 169).
Here Tolkien's recurrent theme of evil arising from desire
for material things is coupled with the theme of the power
of the spoken word. The oath at work was that of Fëanor
and his sons who swore to recover the Silmarils or consign
themselves to the Outermost Dark.

The power of words figures strongly in *The Lord of the Rings.* Gandalf uses spells, lighting fire on Caradhras and at the attack of the wolves by the power of words. He speaks of knowing some two hundred opening spells at the gates of Moria. Gandalf knew shutting spells as well, and spoke of using a Word of Command to lock the door of the Chamber of Mazarbul in Moria. Even the Balrog hesitated at Gandalf's words at the Bridge of Khazad-dûm.

There were powerful oaths in Middle-earth as well as in the West. The Oathbreakers who had broken sworn fealty to Isildur had been reduced to shades—they could find rest only when they renewed and fulfilled their oath to Isildur's heir.

Like Yavanna, Galadriel "sang of trees, of trees of gold, and trees of gold there grew," apparently producing the unique mallorn trees through song.

Prophecies were made, from those of Malbeth the Seer to the prescience of Sam, who "knew he had something to do before the end." But the most powerful words are those of Tolkien himself who made Middle-earth come alive in all its vividness.

Language reflects culture. The hobbits seem, for the most part, rustic country folk. The northern Dúnedain are comparable to the remnants of the Western Roman Empire before its rebirth under Charlemagne. The realm of Gondor is more similar to the Eastern Roman Empire at Constantinople, crumbling but displaying a vestige of past glory. (The siege of Minas Tirith is in fact comparable at many points to the siege of Constantinople in 1453.) The Elves are a living memory of ages beyond the imagination of man. Vocabularies for ruling and military ranks, names that reflect past glories, songs rich in tradition establish much of the culture of the men and Elves at the time of the War of the Ring.

There is another side to Tolkien's linguistic scholarship, one that provides comic relief in jokes, bilingual puns, and linguistic subtleties included for Tolkien's own amusement and that of his colleagues. He poked fun at himself when he said in *Farmer Giles of Ham,* "The parson was a grammarian, and could doubtless see farther into the future than others."

One element of this humor is the suggestion that the mythology, poetry, and even the proverbs of Middle-earth are faintly, and usually incorrectly, recalled in those of historic literature. The story of Ëarendil may be supposed to have been worn down until only the Scandinavian version of the tale of Orentil remains. Our "Hey, diddle diddle, the cat and the fiddle" is supposed to be a poorly remembered version of the song Frodo sang at the inn at Bree. Where Goldberry says, "Make haste while the sun shines," we say "make hay."

Some of Tolkien's intricate puns occur in the evolution of hobbit weekday names from the Elvish. For example, *Alduya* 'day of the two trees' becomes Trewsday: Tuesday.

Another intriguing element of Tolkien's languages is the bilingual meaning of words. Tolkien makes it clear that *Orthanc,* the tower of Saruman, has one meaning, 'cunning mind', in the Old English of Rohan, and another, 'mount fang', in Sindarin Elvish. However, there are other cases. *Athelas* has the Eldarin element *las* 'leaf', although the word is the plural of Old English *athel* 'noble'. Galdor, an Elf of the Gray Havens, has a name meaning 'Shining Lord' in his language but 'enchantment' in Old English. Eärendil, as we have seen, means 'light', 'the first dawn' in Old English, but in Quenya means 'Lover of the Sea'.

Mordor in Old English means 'murder', 'torment', 'mortal sin'. In Elvish it means 'Black Country'. This phrase held personal meaning for Tolkien, who at an early age had to leave the green countryside he loved for Birmingham, in what is called the Black Country—polluted, industrialized, blackened with coal, *Mordor* indeed.

Avallonë, the city of the Elves on Eressëa near Valinor, is likewise reminiscent of Avilon, the island to which King Arthur was said to be taken to be cured of his mortal wounds. Worse, *Akallabêth,* 'the Downfallen', referring to Númenor, is translated into Quenya using the element *lanta* 'fall'. This forms *Atalantë,* making one wonder for a moment whether *The Akallabêth* is the longest buildup to a pun in literature.

Tolkien's invented words often indicate their meaning through sound. Part of this is done by onomatopoeia, the device of making a word sound like the thing named—for example, *sul* and *hwesta,* 'wind' and 'breeze', and *lalaith,* 'laughter'. At other times, consciously or unconsciously, Tolkien chooses words which sound to some extent like their English equivalents. *Mumak* 'Oliphaunt' is similar to *mammoth. Ruth* 'anger' sounds like *wrath,* and *ngol* 'wisdom', 'lore', sounds like *knowledge.*

Using Elvish

It is possible to write or speak original, meaningful, grammatically correct Eldarin sentences. However, use of the language is circumscribed by the size of Tolkien's recorded vocabulary. It is certain that he knew more than was published, but it is doubtful that he ever created enough vocabulary for a living language, even for the expression of the nonhuman concepts of the Elves.

Working within the scope of the vocabulary that exists, we cannot reconstruct the grammar and usage of Elvish without some guesswork. Nevertheless, some useful generalizations can be made.

Quenuvalye i lamber Eldareva.
Thou canst speak the tongues of the Elves.

Verbs

About sixty verbs are given. Generalizing from the tenses given, it is possible to conjugate each Quenya verb in five tenses, singular and plural, and with three pronoun suffixes (*I, we,* and *thou*). In Sindarin six verb tenses are known, but the only pronoun suffix used is *I.*

Note that *tirith* 'watching', 'guard', *sirith* 'a flowing', and *girith* 'shuddering' are nouns and adjectives, not verbs.

*

The following are the verbs in the tenses in which they appear in Tolkien's works.

QUENYA

root forms

kel go away, flow away, flow down
khil follow
kir, cir cut, cleave
lin(d) sing, make a musical sound
pel go around, encircle
quen, quet say, speak
ran wander, stray
rig twine, wreathe
ris cleave
sil shine with a white or silver light
sir flow
tel finish, be last, end
tin(t) sparkle
tir watch, watch over
ur heat, be hot

present	**hypothetical roots**
aiya behold	*aiy*
auta is passing	*aut*
laita praise	*lait*
lantar fall (plural)	*lant*
lintulinda swiftly sing	*lin*
ná is	*n*

present	**hypothetical roots**
nalla cry	*nal*
sila shines	*sil*
tintilar twinkle (plural)	*tintil* from *tin*
untupa down-roofs, covers	*untup*
utúlien I am come	*tul*

imperative

ele behold!	*el*
laite praise!	*lait*

past

avanier have passed away (plural)	*van*
ortane lifted up	*ortan* from *tan*
undulave down-licked, drowned	*undulav, lav =* lick
utúlie'n has come	*tul*
utuvienyes I have found it (with pronoun suffix)	*utuv, yes =* it

future

enquantuva will refill	*enquant* from *quant*
enteluva shall come again	*entel* from *tul*
hiruva will find	*hir*
hiruvalye thou wilt find (with pronoun suffix)	*hir*
laituvalmet we will praise (with pronoun suffix)	*lait*
maruvan I will abide (with pronoun suffix)	*mar*

subjunctive

nai may it be	*n*

SINDARIN

present	hypothetical roots
na is	*n*
penna slants down	*pen*
nallon I cry (with pronoun suffix)	*nal*

imperative

cuio live!	*cui*
daro halt!	*dar*
edro open!	*edr*
eglerio glorify!	*egler* from *aglar*
lasto listen!	*last*
noro ride!	*nor*
pedo speak!	*ped*
tiro watch!	*tir*

participial

díriel after having gazed	*dir*
míriel sparkling like jewels	*mir*
palandiriel gazing afar	*dir*

past

echant made	*ech*
teithant drew	*teith*
onen I gave (with pronoun suffix)	*on*

auxiliary

úchebin I have not kept (with pronoun suffix)	*cheb* = keep

future

linnathon I will chant (with pronoun suffix)	*lin*

miscellaneous
aglarn'i glorify?
ambartanen doomed?
dan take?

If it is hypothesized that these verbs are regular, the following forms can be generalized. The tense, its construction, and two examples are given.

QUENYA

present	past	future
root+*a*	root+*e*	root+*uva*
na is	*ne* was	*nuva* will be
sila shines	*sile* shone	*siluva* will shine

imperative	subjunctive
root+*e*	root+ai
ne be!	*nai* may it be
sile shine!	*silai* may it shine

The plural of each of the tenses above may be formed by adding *r*. When the subject of the sentence is plural, the verb must be plural: e.g., *lassi lantar* leaves fall

present plural	past plural	future plural
nar are	*ner* were	*nuvar* will be
silar shine	*siler* shone	*siluvar* will shine

imperative plural	subjunctive plural
ner be!	*nair* may they be
siler shine!	*silair* may they shine

To indicate the pronouns *I, we,* and *thou* as subjects, the following suffixes are added: *-n* for I, *-(l)met* for we, and *lye* for thou. In the case of *met,* the *l* may take the place of the plural *r*.

present
nan I am
nalmet we are
nalye thou art
silan I shine
silalmet we shine
silalye thou shinest

past
nen I was
nelmet we were
nelye thou wert
silen I shone
silelmet we shone
silelye thou didst shine

future
nuvan I will be
nuvalmet we will be
nuvalye thou wilt be
siluvan I will shine
siluvalmet we will shine
siluvalye thou wilt shine

imperative
nen I am!
nelmet we are!
nelye thou art!
silen I shine!
silelmet we shine!
silelye thou shinest!

subjunctive
nain may it be I
nailmet may it be we
nailye may it be thou
silain may I shine
silailmet may we shine
silailye mayest thou shine

SINDARIN

present	**past**	**future**
root+*a*	root+*ant*	root+*ath*
na is	*nant* was	*nath* will be
edra open	*edrant* opened	*edrath* will open

imperative	**participial**	**auxiliary**
root+*o*	root+*iel*	root+*i*
no be!	*niel* being	*ni* have been
edro open!	*edriel* opening	*edri* have opened

To indicate that the pronoun I is the subject, a vowel and *n* are added, as follows.

present	**past**
root+*on*	root+*en*
non I am	*nen* I was
edron I open	*edren* I opened

future	**auxiliary**
root+*ath*+*on*	root+*in*
nathon I will be	*nin* I have been
edrathon I will open	*edrin* I have opened

Judging from the single example *linnathon* 'I will chant', from the root *lin,* it seems that in this form of the future tense, if there is a single final consonant, it is doubled. If there are two or more final consonants as in *edr,* there is no further change.

Nouns

COMPOUND WORDS

Compound words in both Quenya and Sindarin are usually formed by placing the describing element before the main element, unlike English. The concepts *of* or *of the* are expressed by word order, not by separate syllables.

> *Dúnadan* 'Man of the West' literally 'west-man'
> *Yavanna* 'Giver of Fruits' literally 'fruit-gift'
> *Elendil* 'Lover of the Stars' literally 'star-lover'
> *elanor* 'sun-star' literally 'star-sun'
> *ithildin* 'star-moon' literally 'moon-star'

New compounds can be constructed in this way, as follows.

Gormegil 'Sword of Horror'
Anariel 'Daughter of the Sun'
Arthgon 'Commander of the Realm'
Noldothrond 'Halls of Knowledge'

It is permissible to combine Quenya and Sindarin elements. Tolkien said the name *Boromir* was such a combination. In fact, it is difficult in the majority of cases to know to which language Elvish words belong.

NOUN FORMS

As does Finnish, upon which it is based, Quenya constructs grammatical forms by adding a number of endings. The dual form discussed in this section was also probably inspired by the dual form in Finnish.

Quenya plural is formed by adding *i* to words ending in one or more consonants: *elen, eleni; las, lassi, mir, miri.* Quenya words ending in vowels add *r* to become plurals: *alda, aldar; fana, fanyar; sinda, sindar.*

The Quenya possessive is formed by dropping the final vowel, if any, and adding *o: Varda, Vardo* 'Varda's'; *Calacirya, Calaciryo* 'Calacirya's'. Add *-on* to plurals and do not drop the final vowel: *Silmarillion* 'of the Silmarils', *aldaron* 'of the trees'.

Prepositional elements come at the end of Quenya words, but the final vowel is not dropped: *Oiolosse, Oiolosseo* 'from Everwhite'; *Sindanori, Sindanoriello* 'from gray country'; *Lórien, Lóriendesse* 'in Lórien'.

In Quenya, the dual element is formed by adding *t: maryat* 'hands-her-two', *met* 'us two'.

Sindarin plurals are formed by changing the vowels, as shown below.

adan = man, *edain* = men
amon = hill, *emyn* = hills
annon = gate, *ennyn* = gates
aran = king, *erain* = kings
barad = tower, *beraid* = towers
dan = wright, *dain* = wrights
mallorn = gold-tree, *mellyrn* = gold-trees
Onod = Ent, *Enyd* = Ents
orch = Orc, *yrch* = Orcs
orod = mountain, *ered* = mountains
ras = horn, *rais* = horns

Some of the rules covering these changes are: stressed *a* becomes *e,* unstressed *a* becomes *ai, o* becomes *e, i,* or *y.*

Collective plurals (that is, plurals that signify all of a set of things) are formed in Sindarin by adding *-ath,* or, usually in the case of peoples, *-rim,* literally meaning 'a host,' 'a great number'; *elenath* 'all the stars', *pheriannath* 'the whole race of halflings', *Galadrim* 'all the Tree-folk', *Rohirrim* 'all the Masters of Horses'.

An augmentive suffix, *-on,* is added to Sindarin nouns to signify that the thing is very great or mighty, as in *aearon* 'great sea'.

Sentence Structure

QUENYA

Quenya sentences can have the form subject-verb-object:

hísië untupa Calaciryo míri
mist covers Calacirya's jewels

object-verb-subject:

> *tier undulávë lumbulë*
> roads drowned (by) heavy shadow

or object-subject-verb:

> *máryat Elentari ortanë . . .*
> her two hands Star-queen lifted up . . .

A verb only occurs at the end of a sentence if it is a question:

> *Sí man i yulma nin enquantuva?*
> Now who the cup for me will refill?

Sentences beginning with verbs seem to be emotionally charged:

> *Nai hiruvalye Valimar.*
> May it be that thou shalt find Valimar.
> *Auta i lome!*
> Passing is the night!

If there are one or more nouns before a verb, one of them is usually the subject:

> *Yéni ve lintë yuldar avánier.*
> *Years* like swift draughts have passed away.

However, if the noun before the verb has a prepositional suffix (*-o, -ello, -esse,* 'from,' 'in') the subject will be the noun following the verb:

> *sindanóriello caita mornië i falmalinnar*
> from grey country lies *darkness* the waves upon

Most adjectives precede the noun:

lintë yuldar, lissi miruvoreva
swift draughts, sweet nectar

Adjectives of plural nouns must be plural. Plural adjectives are formed by changing the final vowel to *e* or adding *e*.

SINDARIN

Sindarin sentences can have the form object-verb-subject:

le linnathon
(to) thee chant-will-I (here the subject pronoun is a suffix to the verb)

verb-object:

na vedui Dúnadan
(it) is (at) last Dúnadan

verb-subject:

noro lim, Asfaloth!
ride on, Asfaloth!

subject-verb-object:

Naur dan i ngaurhoth!
Fire take the werewolves!

Verbs are usually followed by their modifiers, which may even come at the end of the sentence:

Cuio i Pherian annan!
Live the Halflings long!

Nouns are usually followed by their modifiers:

Annon edhellen, Fennas nogothrim
Door (of the) Elves, Gateway (of) Dwarf-folk

The concepts 'of' and 'of the' are usually implied by word order, as above. Where 'from' or 'of' is stated, the Sindarin word *o* stands alone, rather than being a suffix, as in Quenya:

o menel,   Celebrimbor o Eregion
from heaven, Celebrimbor of Hollin

QUENYA AND SINDARIN

In the evolution of Quenya and Sindarin from a common primeval language, they diverged in grammar, vocabulary, and sound. One linguist[*] has concluded from the differences in sound (discernible in the following list) that Sindarin was more elegant and melodic because it preferred fronted sounds (those produced more in the front of the mouth) and continuants (sounds that have longer duration, as *th* compared with *t*).

Quenya	Sindarin	translation	comment
coirë,	*echuir,*	stirring,	Many Sindarin words
pel	*ephel*	fence	begin with a vowel which is absent in Quenya. Quenya words, unlike Sindarin, very often end with vowels
carne	*caran*	red	In these words the order of the final vowel and consonant is changed in S to vowel-consonant
alcar	*aglar*	glory	Q *c* becomes S *g* and the order of the consonants is reversed

*Dr. Thomas Donahue, professor of linguistics at San Diego State University.

coirë	*echuir*	stirring	Q *c* becomes S *ch* when it is the first letter
certar, cir	*gerthas, gir*	runes, ship	Q *c* becomes S *g*
dol	*dhol*	head	Q *d* becomes S *dh* when it is the first letter
arda	*arth*	realm, earth	Q *d* becomes S *th* after a consonant
leuca	*lyg*	snake	Q *eu* becomes S *y*
ando	*annon*	gate	Q *nd* becomes S *nn* between vowels
pel, perian	*ephel, pherian*	fence, halfling	Q *p* becomes S *ph*
amrun	*rhûn*	east	Q *r* becomes S *rh*
isil	*ithil*	moon	Q *s* becomes S *th*
mar	*bar*	home	Q *m* becomes S *b*
tin, tar	*din, dor*	spark, lord	Q *t* becomes S *d* when it is the first letter
nor	*dor*	land	Q *n* becomes S *d*
certar	*certhas*	runes	Q *t* becomes S *th* after a consonant
quarë	*bor, paur*	fist	Q *q* becomes S *b* or *p*
viresse	*gwirith*	April	Q *v* becomes S *gw* before *i*
valar	*balar*	powers	Q *v* becomes S *b* before *a*
yanta	*iant*	bridge	Q *y* becomes S *i*

Further similarities and differences in Quenya and Sindarin can be seen in their words for days, months, and seasons.

Quenya	Sindarin	Translation
Elenya	*Orgilion*	Starsday
Anarya	*Oranor*	Sunday
Isilya	*Orithil*	Moonday
Alduya	*Orgaladhad*	Treesday

Aldea	*Orgaladh*	White-tree-day (Númenorean usage)
Menelya	*Ormenel*	Heavensday
Earenya	*Oraearon*	Seaday (Númenorean usage)
Valanya	*Orbelain*	Valarsday
Tarion	*Rodyn*	Powersday (alternate name for Valarsday)
Narvinyë	*Narwain*	January
Nénimë	*Nínui*	February (watery)
Sulimë	*Gwaeron*	March (windy)
Víressë	*Gwirith*	April
Lótessë	*Lothron*	May (in blossom)
Nárië	*Norui*	June (sunny)
Cermië	*Cerveth*	July
Urimë	*Urui*	August (hot)
Yavannië	*Ivanneth*	September (giver of fruits)
Narquellië	*Narbeleth*	October (sun-waning)
Hísimë	*Hithui*	November (misty)
Ringarë	*Girithron*	December (cold-day, shuddering)
tuilë	*ethuil*	spring
lairë	*laer*	summer (green, bright?)
yávië	*iavas*	autumn (fruitful)
quellë	*firith*	fading
lasselanta		leaf-fall
	narbeleth	sun-waning
hrívë	*rhîw*	winter
coirë	*echuir*	stirring

English-to-Elvish
Glossary

Language Code

B Black Speech
C Common Speech (Westron)
D Dunlending
H Hobbit (words other than Westron or ancient English)
K Khuzdul (Dwarvish)
M Any one of the languages of Men
N Númenorean (Adunaic)
O Orkish
PN Pre-Númenorean (Language in the area of Gondor before the coming of the Númenoreans)
Q Quenya
R Rohan
S Sindarin
Sv Sylvan
W Wose

NOTE: A primeval Elvish, or Proto-Quenya, is referred to, but the few words so specified are listed under Quenya with an additional note. Also, in *The Silmarillion* many mortals are named, but unless specified, it is difficult to tell if their names are in one of several early human languages or in Sindarin.

Verb roots are preceded by *to,* as in 'to abide'. The tenses of these verbs should be developed as shown in the preceding chapter. English equivalents of Elvish words are given in Part III, The Tolkien Dictionary.

abhorrence deloth
abhorrent *Q* saur, *S* thaur
to abide *Q* mar
abominable *Q* saur, *S* thaur
abroad *S* palan
abyss iâ
across, *S* thar, *S* thrad
afar *S* palan
again *Q* en-
air *Q* vilya, *Q* wilya
alas *Q* ai
all (plural) *Q* ilye
the all *Q* ilúve
alone, er
and *S* a, *Q* ar
anger rûth
as *Q* ve
ash *S* lith
augmentive prefix to L *S* g-
augmentive suffix *S* -on
autumn *S* iavas, *Q* yávië
awakening *Q* coire, cuivië, *S* echoir, echui

awe, gaya
axes, *K* baruk

bald *S* rûdh
bane dagnir
barrow *S* tûr, *plural* tyrn
battle dagnir, ndak, dagor
to be *Q, S* n-
be it that *Q* nai
beard fan(g)
beautiful (fair) *Q* vana
because (for) *Q* an
beech neldor
to behold *Q* aiy-, *Q* el-
to bend lok
beside *Q* ar
between *S* im, *Q* imbe
beyond *Q* pella
birch *S* brethil
bird (small) *S* aew, *Q* aiwë
black mor, vorn
blessed aman, man
blood agar, *S* sereg, *Q* serke
bloodstained agarwaen
blossom *N* inzil, *Q* lótë, *S* loth
blue *S* lhun, *S* luin, *Q* luinë
book *Q* parma
bow cú, *Q* lúva
breeze *Q* hwesta
bridge *S* iant, *Q* yanta
brilliance *S* ril, *Q* rildë, *Q* rillë
bull mundo
butterfly *Q* wilwarin

cave grod, groth, rod
chambers *S* sammath
champion *Q* aráto
to chant *S* lin
children *Q* hini, *S* hîn
chill *S* ring
to cleave cir, kir, ris
cleaver crist, grist, kris, hyando
cleft cir, cirith
cloak *Q* collo, *S* gollo
cloud *S* fan, *S* fân, *Q* fana, *plural* fanyar
coast falas, falath
collective plural suffix *S* -ath, *S* -rim, *Q* rimbë
course rant
cold ring
to come *Q* túl
commander *Q* káno, *S* gon
consumer *Q* vása
cool him
to cover *Q* untup-
crow *S* craban, *S plural* crebain
to cry *Q, S* nall-
cup *Q* yulma
to cut cir, kir

dark *B* burz, *S* dûr, mor
darkness *B* burzum, *S* fuin, *Q* huine, *Q* mornië
daughter *Q,S* -iel
dauntless *S* thalion
day *S* -or, *Q* ré
dead *S* firn
death *S* gurth
deep *Q* balë, *Q* búlë

demon *S* raug, *Q* rauko, *S* rog
devoted to (n)dil, (n)dur, nil, nur
dimness *S* du, *S* gwath, *S* wath, *S* weth
direction *Q* men
dog (great) huan
dome *Q* telluma, *plural* tellumar
doom *S* amarth, *Q* ambar, *Q* umbar
door *S* annon, *plural* ennyn, *S* fen, *S* fennas
double adu
down *Q* ndu, *Q* nu
to down-lick *Q* undulav-
to down-roof *Q* untup-
draught *Q* yulda, *plural* yuldar
to draw *S* teith-
dread gaya, *S* gor, *S* goroth
to drown *Q* undulav-
dusk *S* dōmē *Q* lómë, *S* moth
Dwarf *K* Khazâd *S* naug, *plural* naugrim, *S* nog, *S* nogoth, *plural* noegyth
Dwarvish language *K* Khuzdul
to dwell *Q* mar-
dwelling *S* bar, *Q* mar

eagle *Q* soron, *S* thoron
ear *S* lhaw
earth *Q* arda, *Q* kemen
east *S* rhûn, *Q* rôm, *Q* romen, *S* rûn
echo lóm
echo (great) lammoth
Elf *S* edhel, *plural* edhil, *Q* elda, *plural* eldar, *S* eledh, *Q* quendi
empty lost
to encircle *Q* pel

encircling wall *S* echor
end met
to end *Q* tel
Ent *S* Onod, *plural* Onodrim or Enyd
to enter *S* minn-
even thou *Q* elye
ever *Q* oi, *S* oiale, *Q* oio, *S* ui
exalted *Q* varda
eye *S* hen

fading *S* beleth, *S* firith, *Q* quelle
fair-haired *Q* vana
to fall *Q* lanta
fangs *S* carach, *S* carag, *S* carak, *S* carch, *Q* caraxë, *Q* carca
far *Q* hae
far and wide *Q, S* palan
far-seer *Q* palantir, *plural* palantiri
farewell *Q* namárië
fate *Q* ambar, *Q* umbar, *S* amarth
father *Q* atar, *S* adar
feast mereth
feather *Q* quesse
fell (adjective) aeg
feminine name suffix -iel
fence *S* iâth
fence (outer) *S* ephel
to fill *Q* quant-
to find *Q* hir, *Q* utuv-
figure *Q* fana
to finish *Q* tel
fire *B* ghâsh, *Q* nar, *S* naur
first *Q* minya

fist *S* paur, *Q* quárë
flame (leaping) lach, lhach
flame (red) *S* ruin, *Q* runya
flat-lands *S* talath
flow *S* dui
to flow *Q* sir
to flow away, to flow down *Q* cel, *Q* kel
flower *N* inzil, *Q* lótë, *S* loth, *Q* lot
flowing sirith
foam rhos, ros, roth, ving, wing
to follow *Q* khil, hil
foot *S* dal, *Q* tal
for (because) *Q* an
ford athrad, iach
forest *S* erin, *plural* eryn, *S* taur, *Q* taurë
forsaken egla
fortress ost
friend (n)dil, (n)dur, nil, nur, *S* mellon
from *Q* -ello, *Q* -o
from on high *Q* ndu
fruit *Q* yávë

gape faug
gate *Q* ando, *S* annon, *plural* ennyn, *S* fen, *S* fennas
garlanded maiden *Q* -riel
to gaze *S* dir, *Q* tir
to gaze afar *S* palandir
gazing *S* diriel
gift *Q* anna
to give *S* on-
glass *S* heled, *K* kheled
gleam glîn
glittering bril

glittering white *S* silivren
gloom *S* fuin, *Q* huinë
gloomy dim
glory *S* aglar, *Q* alcar, *Q* alkar
glorious *S* aglareb, *Q* alcarin, alkarinque
to go around *Q* pel
to go away *Q* cel, *Q* kel
goblin *S* glam, *plural* glamhoth, *S* orch, *plural* yrch, *B* uruk, *B* uruk-hai
gold *S* mal, *plural* mel, *Q* malta, *N* pharaz
gold (color or light) *S* glor, *S* lor, *Q* laurë
golden *Q* laurëa, *Q* laurië
golden-brown *S* baran
golden-red cul
good mān
grade *Q* tyelle, *plural* tyeller
gravel *S* brith
gray *S* mith, *S* thin(d), *Q* sinda
green *S* calen, *S* galen, *plural* gelin, *Q* lai
growth loa

hair fin
half *Q* per, *S* pher
hall with arched roof rond, thrond
hall *Q* mard, *plural* mardi
to halt *S* dar-
hammer *S* dring
hand *S* bor, *S* cam, *S* cham, *Q* kambā, *Q* ma, *Q* maite, *Q* quarë
harbor, haven *S* lonn, *S* lond, *Q* londe
head dhol, dol
hearing *S* lhaw
heart *Q* orë

heat *Q* ur
heaven *Q, S* menel
heavy blung
heir *S* chil, *S* réd, *Q* hil, *plural* hildinyar
helm thôl
here *S* si
hidden *S* dolen
hiding esgal
high ar(a), arat, don, *Q* oro, *Q* tan, *Q* tar, *Q* tára
hill *S* amon, *plural* emyn
hither nev
hollow *S* nov
a hollow *Q* unque
holly ereg, reg
holy *Q* aina, *Q* aire
home *S* bar, *Q* mar
hook *Q* ampa
hope *S* estel
horn *S* dil, *S* ras, *plural* rais, *Q* til
horror del, *S* gor, *S* goroth
horde *S* hoth
horse *S* roch, *S* ro(h), *Q* rokko
host *S* hoth, *S* rim, *Q* rimbë
to be hot *Q* ur
hound huan
hour lúmenn'
howl ngwaw
hunt faroth

I *S* im
ice *S* khelek
icy, ice-cold *Q* helka
in *Q* -esse

in the *Q* mí
in this place *Q* sinome
in which *Q* yassen
iron *S* ang, *Q* anga
of iron *S* angren, *plural* engrin
is *Q, S* na
island tol
it *Q* -yes

jaws *Q* anca, carka, *S* carach, carag, carak
jewel *S* mîr, *Q* mírë

to keep *S* cheb-
kindler *S* thoniel
king *S* aran, *plural* erain or erein
knowledge *S* golodh, *Q* noldo, *Q* nólë

lady *S* híril
lair torech
lake aelin, lin
lamp *Q* calma
lament *Q* dénië, *Q* nainië
land *S* dór, (n)dor, nor, *Q* nórë
last *S* vedui
to be last *Q* tel-
laughter lalaith
lawn *S* parth
leaf *Q* asea, las, *plural* lassi
letter *Q* tengwa, *plural* tengwar, *S* tîw
to lie *Q* cait-
life coi
to lift up *Q* ortan-
light *Q* cal, *Q* kal, *S* galad

like *Q* ve
to live *S* cui-, *S* guin-
to listen *S* last-
lofty don, *S* tar, *Q* tára
lonely ereb
long an, and, anann
look toward *S* tir
loop lok
lord *Q* heru, *S* hir, *K* uzbad
lore *Q* nólë
lost *Q* vanwa
love mel
lover of (n)dil, (n)dur, nil, nur

to make *S* ech-
maiden ien, -wen
maiden (garlanded) riel
man *S* adan, *plural* edain, *Q* atan, *plural* atani
masculine name suffix -ion
mastery tur
may it be *Q* nai
me-for *Q* nin
meeting (of our) omentielvo
mesh rem, rembe, rembre
metal *Q* tinco
middle en, ened
mighty beleg
mind *Q* ore
mist *Q* his, *Q* hísië, *S* hith
month *Q* asta, *plural* astar
moon *Q* isil, *S* ithil
mortal fir
mound cerin, corol, coron, *S* haudh, *S* tûr, *plural* tyrn

mountain *S* orod, *plural* ered
mouth *Q* anto

name *Q* esse
near nev
nectar miruvor
net rim, rembe, rembre
new vinya
night *S* dú
nightingale *S* dúlin, *S* tinuviel, *Q* lómelindë, *Q* tindomerel
noble ar, ara, arat
noise (din) glam
north *S* for, *S* forn, *S* forod, *Q* formen
not *Q, S* ú-
now *Q* si
number (great) *S* rim, *Q* rimbë

O! *S* a!
ocean *S* aear, *Q* ëar
of *Q* -ello, *Q* -eva, *Q, S* -o, *K* -ul
old iar, iaur
old man *B* sharkû
oliphaunt mûmak, *plural* mûmakil
on this side of *S* nef
one *B* ash, *Q* er
to open *S* edr-
oppression *S* thang
out et, eth
outflow ethir
outside *Q* ar

pass cirith
to pass *Q* aut-, *Q* van-

people *Q* nórë, *S* waith
petty *S* nibin
pillar tarma
pine *S* thôn
place (in this) *Q* sinome
plain lad, talath
platform talan
plural collective suffix *S* -ath, *S* -rim
point ae, *S* dil, *Q* til
pool aelin, lin
power *S* bal, *plural* bel, *S* rod, *plural* rodyn, *Q* tur, *Q* val
to praise *S* egl-, *Q* lait-
prince ernil
prison *S* band, *Q* mando, *Q* mbando
pursue faroth

queen *S* bereth, *Q* tári

radiance *Q* alata, *S* galad
rage *Q* aha
rain *Q* ulma
rainbow ninniach
ransom danwedh
re- *Q* en-
red *S* car, caran, *Q* carnë
to refill *Q* enquant-
refuser avar
region *Q* arda, *Q* men, *S* arth
remembrance -rín
rest *Q* este
reversed *Q* nuquerna
to ride *S* nor-
ridges *S* pinnath
ring *Q* cor, *B* nazg

ringwraith *B* nazgûl
river *S* duin, *S* duinë, *S* hir, *Q, S* sîr, *Q* luinë
roads *Q* tier
root thond
royal ar, ara, arat
rune *Q* certa, *plural* certar, *S* certhas, *S* cirth, *S* gerthas
rushing alag, alak, asca

sad dim
to say *S* ped-, *Q* quen- *Q* quet-
screen esgal
sea *S* ae, *S* aer, *S* gaer, *Q* ëar
series *Q* tema, *plural* temar
serpent *Q* hlokë, *Q* lokë, *S* lhug, *S* lyg
seven *S* odo, *Q* otso
shadow *S* ath, *S* dae, *S* gwath, *S* wath, *S* weth
shadow (heavy) *Q* lumbule
shadows cast by light morchaint
sharp *S* maeg, *Q* maika
to shine *Q* cal-, *Q* kal-, *S* gal-
to shine with white or silver light *Q* sil-, *S* thil-
ship cair, cir, cirya, gir
shore falas, falath, rast, rest
shuddering girith
sickly engwa
sign *Q* tehta, *S* thîw
silent dín
silver *S* celeb, *Q* telep, *Q* telpë
silver-like *S* celebrin, *Q* telperin
to sing *Q, S* lin-
singer lindë
skill curu
sky *Q* vilya, *Q* wilya

to slant down *S* penn-
slave *B* snaga
slender, slim fim
snake *Q* hlokë, *Q* lokë, *Q* leuca, *S* lhûg, *plural* lyg
snow *Q, S* loss, *Q* lossë
snowy lossen
son of *Q, S* -ion, *K* -ul
sorcery morgûl, *S* gûl
south *S* har, *S* harad, *S* harn, *Q* hyarmen
spark *S* gil, *Q* tinwë
to sparkle *S* din-, *Q, S* tin-, *Q* it-, *Q* tint-, *Q* tintil-
to sparkle like jewels *S* mír-
to speak *S* ped-, *Q* quen-, *Q* quet-
spider ungol
spider web *Q* ungwe
spirit *Q* fëa, *Q* sulë, *Q* thulë
spindrift, spray ros, rhos, ving, wing
spring of water *Q* et-kelé, *Q* etelë, *S* eithel
spring season *S* ethuil, *Q* tuilë
stake *S* ceber, *plural* cebir, *S* gebir
star *Q, S* el, *Q* elen, *plural* eleni, *S* elen, *plural* elenath
    or elin, *S* gil, il
star-host *S* giliath
starlight *Q* silme
stars (of the) elda, *plural* eldar, elena
stem *Q* telco
stirring *Q* coire, *S* echuir
stone *S* gon, *S* gond, *Q* ondo
stone (small) sarn, *plural* serni
to stray raen-, ran-
stream hir, sir
street *S* rath
strong *S* thalion

sudden bragol
surfline falas, falath
summer *S* laer, *Q* laire
sun *Q* anar, *S* anor
sunlight *Q* árë, *Q* ázë, *S* aur, *S* aurë
sunrise *Q* romen, *S* rûn
sunset *Q* andúnê, *S* annûn
swan *S* alph, *Q* alqua
sweet *Q* lissi
swift *Q* linte
sword *S* megil, *Q* macil
swordsman *Q* macar, *S* vagor

tall *Q* halla
the *Q* i
thee *Q* le
them *S* hain
these *S* hin
this *S* hi
thorn ereg, reg
thou *Q* lye, *S* le
thou (even) *Q* elye
thousand mene
thread *S* lain
three neldë
throng *Q* sanga
to thee *S* le
tongue *Q* lambe
tower *S* barad, *plural* beraid, *B* lug, *Q,S* minas
torment *Q* ngwalme, *Q* nwalme, *Q* ywalme
torrent *S* thor
treasure *Q* harma
tree *Q* alda, *plural* aldar, *S* galadh, *plural* galadhad, *S* orn

troll *B* olog, *S* torog
trumpet sound rom
twilight aduial, minuial, tindome, uial, undome
to twine rig
to twinkle *Q* tintil-

un- *Q* ú-
under *Q* nu, nuin
underground dwelling *S* grod, *S* groth, *S* rod
unto *Q* tenn'
unwilling *Q* avar
us two *Q* met

valiant astaldo
valley *S* dun, nan, nand, imlad, tum, *Q* tumbo
vaulted roof rond
veil *Q,S* fana
victor *Q* dacil
void iâ
voice *S* lammen, *Q* oma

wall *S* ram, *Q* ramba
to wander raen, ran
wanderer randir
to watch, to watch over *Q, S* tir-
water nen
waterfall lanthir
wave (crested) *Q* falma
way *S* bad, *Q* pata
we two *Q* met
week *Q* enquië, *plural* enquier
well of water *Q* ehtelë, *S* eithel
werewolf gaur, ngaur
west *N* adûn, *S* annún, *S* dûn, *Q* númen

wet med, nin
white (dazzling) *S* glos
white *S* nim, nimf, nimp, niph, *Q* ninque
who *Q* man
whole *Q* iluve
will *Q* -uva
willow *Q* tasarë, *S* tathar, *S* tathren
wind *S* gwae, *S* gwai, *Q* súl
window *S* henneth
wing *Q* rama, *plural* ramar
winter *Q* hrivë, *S* hrîw
wise, wisdom *S* golodh, *plural* gelydh, *Q* noldo, *Q* nolë
without *Q* ar
wolf draug
woods *S* erin, *plural* eryn, *S* taur, *Q* taurë
word *S* beth, *Q* quetta
to wreathe rig-
Wose dru
wright *S* dan, *plural* dain

-y *Q* -ime, *S* -ui
year (solar) loa
year (long Elven) *Q* yen, *plural* yeni

PART III

THE TOLKIEN DICTIONARY: FOURTEEN TOLKIEN LANGUAGES

Pronunciation

The following guide is to the pronunciation of the languages of Middle-earth in *The Silmarillion, The Hobbit,* and *The Lord of the Rings.* The guide also covers the Old Norse names of the Dwarves and the Old English personal and place names in Rohan. The words in modern English spelling, such as *Shadowfax,* are to be given modern English pronunciation.

The following information is adapted from the Appendix of *The Silmarillion,* Appendix E of *The Lord of the Rings,* and Tolkien's updated notes on page 63 of *The Road Goes Ever On.*

c   always has the value of *k,* never of *s,* even when followed by *i, e,* or *y. Celeb* 'silver' is pronounced *keleb.* Finnish, the language from which Quenya was devised, does not use the letter *c* except in a few borrowed words such as *Centigrade.* Tolkien retained the Finnish *k* in *The Silmarillion* and in a few cases in *The Lord of the Rings,* such as the river *Kelos.* As he compared the relationship between Quenya and Sindarin to that between Latin and English, he revised the spelling, using the more familiar *c.* Usually the use of *k* became a mark of a language foreign to the Elves, such as Orkish, Khuzdul (Dwarvish), and Adûnaic (Númenorean).

ch   always has the value of *ch* in Scottish *loch* or German *buch,* never that in English *church.* In Orkish and Númenorean, *kh* has this sound.

dh   represents the voiced *th* in *then,* not the unvoiced *th* in *thin.* In some languages, such as Old English, separate letters are used for the voiced and unvoiced *th.* A voiced sound is one in which the speaker can feel vibration in the larynx with the hand pressed to the throat while pronouncing the sound. The voiced *th* occurs in such words as *Haudh, Maedhros,* and *Caradhras.*

f   represents the *f* in *find* except at the end of words, as in English *of.* Note that the root *nef* is spelled with a *v* when used in the compound *Nevrast* 'Hither Shore'.

g   always has the value of *g* in *get, gild,* even when followed by *e, i,* or *y. Gildor* begins as does *Gilbert; Region* begins as does *regulate. Gh* in Black Speech and Orkish is pronounced at the back of the throat, similarly to the *ch* above, but starting with the sound *g.*

h   alone, uncombined with other consonants, has the value of *h* in *house, behold.* It has special values when combined as *ch, dh, lh, rh, th, hw,* and *hy.* In Quenya, *ht* has the value of *cht* in German *acht.* This combination appears in *Telumehtar.*

i   in Sindarin, when occurring at the beginning of a word and followed by another vowel, has the value of the consonant *y* in *you*. Thus *Ioreth* begins as does English *yore*. This is because the Sindarin *y* is used as a vowel only and *i* can take the place of consonant *y*.

k   is usually used in languages other than Elvish and has the sound of *k* in *king*. In Orkish words such as *Grishnakh* and Númenorean words such as *Adûnakhor, kh* has the sound of *ch* given above. In Dwarvish, *k* and *h* are sounded separately, as in *backhand*.

l   has approximately the sound of *l* in *let*. However, between *e* or *i* and a consonant, or after *e* or *i* at the end of a word, *l* was somewhat 'palatalized', that is, pronounced with the blade of the tongue, rather than the tip of the tongue, against the hard palate, as in *Eldar*.

lh   represents an unvoiced, palatalized *l*. In archaic Quenya this was written *hl*.

ng   has the value of *ng* in *finger* except at the beginning and end of words where it has the value of *ng* in *sing*, as in Sindarin *ngaurhoth* 'werewolves'.

qu   has the sound *kw*.

ph   has the sound of *f* in *find*.

r   is trilled in all positions. In Orkish and Dwarvish, the *r* can be pronounced at the back of the throat. *Rh,* or *hr* as it was written in Quenya, represents a voiceless *r*.

s   is always voiceless, as in *so*. The sound *z* as in *is, zoo*, did not occur in Elvish. Where *z* occurs, as in Dwarvish, it has the sound of the English *z*. *Sh* in Westron, Dwarvish, and Orkish is similar to *sh* in English.

th has the value of the voiceless *th* in *thin.* In Dwarvish,
      t and *h* had separate sounds, as in *boathouse.*

ty has the value of the *t* in British *tune,* not the Ameri-
      can "toon." It has some of the quality of the English
      ch, as heard in some English dialect pronunciations
      of *tune* as "chune."

v   has the value of the English *v,* not the German.

w   has the value of the English *w,* not the German. *Hw*
      is a voiceless *w,* as in *white, whale.*

y   in Quenya is used for the consonant sound of *y* in
      you. In Sindarin *y* represented the modified *u* in
      French *lune.* In Old English *y* was used for that
      sound. In Gondor the Sindarin *y* was pronounced
      like the *i* in *sick. Hy* represents a sound similar to
      that in *hew* and *huge,* as in *Hyarmen.* This sound is
      represented by the *h* in Quenya *eht* and *aht.*

Consonants written twice are pronounced long. This
usually occurs in English in compound words. The *m* in
Rammas Echor and *Sammath Naur* have the sound of *m*
in *roommate* rather than that in *ramming.*

a   has the sound in *father.*

e   has the sound in *bed* and is pronounced as a separate
      syllable in the middle of words such as *Merethrond*
      'Feast Hall' and at the end of words such as *lómë*
      'dusk' where it is usually marked ë.

i   has the sound in *sick.*

o   has the sound in *hot,* but 'rounder' than in modern
      English, apparently with the mouth and lips held
      more open.

u   has the sound in *brute* even when long. Túrin is
      pronounced 'Toorin', not 'Tyoorin'.

Long vowels were marked with an acute accent, *á.* These vowels were long in duration rather than having a different sound: not as in *ape* contrasted with *apple.* However, in Quenya, long *é* and *ó* are correctly pronounced with a 'tenser and closer' sound than the short vowels, apparently with the mouth and lips more closed. In Sindarin, stressed one-syllable words are marked with a circumflex accent, indicating a particularly prolonged vowel, as in *dûn,* contrasted with *Dúnadan.* In languages other than Elvish, a vowel with a circumflex accent, as in *Khazad-dûm,* is an ordinary long vowel.

ae and *ai*	have the sound of *eye. Dúnedain* ends with a syllable pronounced *dine.*
ei	has the sound in *gray.*
ie	has the vowels sounded separately and run together, as in *Ni-enna.* It does not have the sound in *piece.*
oe and *oi*	have the sound of the vowels in *boy, toy.*
ui	is pronounced as are the vowels in *ruin,* but run together into one syllable.
au and *aw*	have the sound in *loud* and *how. Sauron* begins with a syllable pronounced *sour.*
er, ir, ur	before a consonant, as in *Cirdan,* or at the end of a word, as in *Ainur,* should be pronounced as in English *air, eer, oor.*
ea and *eo*	are not run together, but form separate syllables. In Rohan, *ea* has the sound in *bear* and *éo* is pronounced as two syllables run together. *Éomer* is pronounced approximately *eh-oh-mare.*

Stress. In two-syllable words the stress or accent is on the first syllable. In longer words it occurs on the next to last syllable if that syllable contains a vowel followed by two or more consonants, a long vowel, or a diphthong (two vowels pronounced in one syllable, such as *ai, ei*). I*sil*dur and Pe*lar*gir are words of this type. If the next to last syllable contains a short vowel followed by one or no consonants, the stress falls on the syllable before it, the third from the end. *Fe*anor, Er*es*sëa, and *Den*ethor are words of this type. Digraphs, pairs of consonants that make a single sound, such as *ch, dh, ph, sh,* and *th,* are counted as one letter in determining stress, and are written with one letter in the Eldarin alphabets.

Codes

In the Tolkien Dictionary, the word is given in boldface, then the code letter of the language, the translation, a brief identification, analysis of compound words, and the code letter of the book and number of the page on which the word is given. The page number is that of the original Houghton Mifflin Company hardcover edition. Readers having a different edition of Tolkien's works will find it simplest to look up persons, places, and things in the index of their edition; they may look up isolated words in the translation of quotations in this book.

Absence of a language code indicates uncertainty as to whether the language is Quenya or Sindarin, or, in the cases of the names of some men, whether the names are in a language of men or in Sindarin.

Translations in single quotation marks are those given by Tolkien himself. Those in parentheses are not specifically given by Tolkien. The process by which they were arrived at, often the analysis of compound words, is given.

Only one page number is shown for most words; it is usually either the page upon which the translation is given or the first page upon which the word occurs.

Language Code

B   Black Speech
C   Common Speech (Westron)
D   Dunlending
H   Hobbit (words other than Westron or ancient English)
K   Khuzdul (Dwarvish)
M   Any one of the languages of Men
N   Númenorean (Adunaic)
O   Orkish
PN Pre-Númenorean (Language in the area of Gondor before the coming of the Númenoreans)
Q   Quenya
R   Rohan
S   Sindarin
Sv Sylvan
W   Wose

NOTE: A primeval Elvish, or Proto-Quenya, is referred to, but the few words so specified are listed under Quenya with an additional note. Also, in *The Silmarillion* many mortals are named, but unless specified, it is difficult to tell if their names are in one of several early human languages or in Sindarin.

Book Code and Bibliography

H   *The Hobbit,* J. R. R. Tolkien, Houghton Mifflin Company, Boston, 1966.

1   *The Fellowship of the Ring,* J. R. R. Tolkien, Houghton Mifflin Company, Boston, 1965.

2   *The Two Towers,* J. R. R. Tolkien, Houghton Mifflin Company, Boston, 1965.

3   *The Return of the King,* J. R. R. Tolkien, Houghton Mifflin Company, Boston, 1965.

A   *The Adventures of Tom Bombadil,* J. R. R. Tolkien, Ballantine Books, New York, 1965.

C   *A Tolkien Compass,* Jared Lobdell, Editor, Open Court, LaSalle, Ill., 1975.

R   *The Road Goes Ever On, A Song Cycle,* Donald Swann and J. R. R. Tolkien, Ballantine Books, New York, 1967.

S   *The Silmarillion,* J. R. R. Tolkien, Houghton Mifflin Company, Boston, 1977.

T   *Tolkien,* Humphrey Carpenter, Houghton Mifflin Company, Boston, 1977.

1/oo The map in *The Fellowship of the Ring.* *

3/oo The map in *The Return of the King.* *

o/oo The map poster by J. R. R. Tolkien, Christopher Tolkien, and Pauline Baynes, 1966.*

(*Wherever these three codes are found, they refer to maps only and will bear no cross-reference page number.)

The Tolkien Dictionary

Note: The words with no page numbers given are forms, such as singular or plural, that do not exist in Tolkien's works and are hypothesized only.

A

a *S* 'and'. 1/319

a *S* 'O!'. R/64

Adan *S* 'man'. R/66

Adanedhel 'Elf Man'. A name of Turin. **Adan** = man, **edhel** = Elf. S/201

Adorn *S* A river tributary to the Isen. **orn** = tree. 3/346

Adrahil *N* A prince of Dol Amroth, father of Imrahil. 3/336

adu 'double'. S/363

aduial *S* 'evendim'. **du** = night, dimness, **uial** = twilight. 3/384

adûn *N* 'west'. Derived from *Q* **númen**. S/355

Adûnaic *N* 'Westron'. The Númenorean language. **adûn** = west. 3/394

Adurant 'Double Stream'. A river. S/123

ae (sea). See **Aerandir** 'Sea Wanderer'.

ae (point). See **Aeglos** 'Snow Point'.

aear *S* 'ocean'. R/64

aearon *S* 'great ocean', 'great sea'. **aear** = ocean, **-on** = augmentive suffix. R/64

aeg (fell) adjective. See **Aegnor** 'Fell Fire'.

Aeglos 'Snow Point'. Spear of Gil-galad, spelled **Aiglos** in *The Lord of the Rings.* S/294

Aegnor 'Fell Fire'. A son of Finarfin. From *Q* **Aikanáro** = (Sharp Flame). S/61

aelin 'lake', 'pool'. S/355

Aelin-uial 'Meres of Twilight'. A series of lakes. **aelin** = lake, pool, **uial** = twilight. S/144

Aerandir 'Sea Wanderer'. A companion of Eärendil. **aear** = ocean, **randir** = wanderer. S/248

Aerin A woman who aided Morwen. **aear** = sea. S/198

aerlinn (chant) The form of song of '*A Elbereth Gilthoniel*', written in *tengwar* script as a subtitle to the song. **lin** = song. R/62

aew 'small bird'. S/361

Agarwaen 'Blood-stained'. A name of Turin. S/210

agh *B* 'and'. 1/267

aglar *S* 'glory'. Compare *Q* **alcar.** R/64

aglareb *S* 'glorious'. S/355

aglar'ni *S* (glorify them). **aglar** = glory. 3/231

Aglarond 'Place of Glory'. The Glittering Caves. **aglar** = glory, **-ond** = place name suffix. 2/145

Aglon A place called the Narrow Pass. S/123

aha *Q* 'rage'. Old name for the Quenya letter *h,* later called **harma** 'treasure'. 3/401

ai *Q* 'alas'. R/58

Aiglos *S* 'Snow Point', 'Icicle'. The spear of Gil-galad, as spelled in *The Lord of the Rings.* **ae** = point, **glos** = dazzling-white, **los** = snow. 1/256

aimênu *K* 'are upon you'. 3/411

aina 'holy'. S/355

Ainu 'Holy One'. Singular form of **Ainur.**

Ainulindale 'The Music of the Ainur'. The music of creation in which the Ainur sang, and the account of that singing. **ainur** = holy ones, **lin** = song, music. S/15

Ainur 'The Holy Ones'. The Valar and Maiar, angelic powers. S/15

aire *Q* 'holy'. R/58

aire-tari *Q* 'holy queen'. **aire** = holy, **tari** = she that is lofty, queen. R/58

aiwë *Q* 'small bird'. S/361

aiya *S* 'behold'. S/190

Akallabêth *N* 'Downfallen'. Compare *Q* **Atalantë.** The name of Númenor after its sinking and the account of the history of Númenor. S/290

alag 'rushing'. S/355

alak 'rushing'. S/355

alata *Q* 'radiance'. S/360

alcar *Q* 'glory'. See *S* **aglar** = glory. R/64

alcarin *Q* 'glorious'. R/65

Alcarinquë *Q* 'The Glorious'. A star. S/48

Alcarondas *N* The ship of Ar-Pharazon, called Castle of the Sea. Compare *Q* **alcar** = glory. S/278

alda *Q* 'tree'. The Quenya letter ld. See **galadh** *S* 'tree'. 3/401

Aldalóme (Tree-shadow). A forest. **alda** = tree, **lóme** = shadow. 2/72

Aldamir *Q* (Tree-jewel). The twenty-second King of Gondor. **alda** = tree, **mir** = jewel. 3/319

aldar *Q* (trees). *See* **aldaron.**

aldaron *Q* 'of trees'. R/58

Aldaron *Q* 'Forester', '(Lord) of Trees'. A name of Oromë. S/29

Aldea *Q* (Tree-day). The day named in honor of the White Tree. 3/388

Aldudénië *Q* 'Lament for the Two Trees'. A song. Compare *Q* **nainië** 'lament'. S/76

Alduya *Q* (Trees-day). The day named in honor of the Two Trees. 3/388

alfirin A golden flower. Compare **fir** = mortal, **firith** = fading. 3/151

alkar *Q* 'glory'. S/355

alkarinquë *Q* 'glorious'. S/355

Almaren An island where the Valar first lived. **mar** = dwelling. S/76

alph *S* 'swan'. 3/392

alqua *Q* 'swan'. S/355

Alqualondë *Q* 'Haven of the Swans'. The city and harbor of the Teleri in the Blessed Realm. **alqua** = swan, **londë** = harbor, haven. S/60

Altariel *Q* 'Maiden Crowned with a Radiant Garland'. The Quenya form of the name Galadriel, referring to her hair. **alata** = radiance, **riel** = garlanded maiden, from **rig** twine, wreathe. S/360

Altariello *Q* 'Galadriel's'. See **Altariel.** **-o** = from, of. R/58

Aman *Q* 'Blessed', 'Free from Evil'. The Blessed Realm. 3/317

Amandil 'Lover of Aman'. The father of Elendil. **dil** = friend, lover of, devoted to. S/271

Amanyar *Q* 'Those of Aman'. The Elves who reached the Blessed Realm, as distinguished from the Umanyar, who did not. S/353

Amarië (Of the Home). An Elf-woman. **mar** = home. S/130

amarth *S* 'doom'. 3/317

ambar *Q* 'doom'. S/355

Ambar-metta *Q* (the end of doom). **met** = end. 3/245

Ambarona *Q* (Land of Doom). **-ona** = place name suffix. 2/27

ambartanen *Q* (doomed). S/223

Amlach A mortal man. **lach** = leaping flame. S/144

Amlaith *S* Of Fornost, second King of Arthedain. 3/318

ammen *S* Adverb in *Naur an edraith ammen* and *Edro hi ammen*. 1/304, 1/312, 1/320

amon *S* 'hill'. Plural **emyn**. 3/393

Amon Amarth *S* 'Mount Doom'. An older name for Orodruin, the Burning Mountain. **amarth** = doom. 3/317

Amon Dîn (Silent Hill). A beacon hill in northern Gondor. **dîn** = silent. 3/19

Amon Ereb 'The Lonely Hill'. In East Beleriand. **ereb** = lonely. S/96

Amon Ethir Called The Hill of Spies; however, elsewhere **ethir,** as in **Ethir Anduin,** means outflow, so the hill may originally have been named for a spring or river. S/217

Amon Gwareth The hill of Gondolin. Compare *S* **Gwirith** (April). S/126

Amon Hen 'Hill of the Eye', 'Hill of Sight'. A hill above Rauros. 1/406

Amon Lhaw 'Hill of Hearing'. A hill above Rauros. 1/405

Amon Obel A hill in the forest of Brethil. S/203

Amon Rûdh 'The Bald Hill'. Home of Mîm the Petty-Dwarf. S/201

Amon Sûl *S* 'Weathertop'. Hill between Bree and Rivendell. **sûl** = wind. 1/197

Amon Uilos *S* 'Mount Everwhite'. In the Blessed Realm. S/37

ampa *Q* 'hook'. The name of the Quenya letter *mp*. 3/401

Amras A son of Fëanor. **ras** = peak, horn. S/60

Amrod A son of Fëanor. **rod** = power. S/60

Amroth *Sv* An Elven King of Lórien who gave his name to Cerin Amroth and Dol Amroth. **roth** = foam. 1/354

amrûn *S* 'east', 'sunrise'. 3/401

an *Q* 'for', 'because'. R/58

an(d) 'long'. S/355

Anach A pass from Dorthonion. **an** = long. S/200

Anadûnê *N* 'Westernesse'. Númenor. S/261

anann (long). 3/231

(a)nar *Q* 'fire'. An ancient root word both for **nor,** fire, and **anar,** sun. S/362

Anar *Q* 'sun', 'The Fire-Golden'. S/99

Anardil *Q* (Lover of the Sun). The fifth King of Gondor. **dil** = friend, lover of, devoted to. 3/318

Anárion *Q* (Sun, Lord of the Sun). The son of Eärendil and first King of Gondor. **-ion** = masculine name suffix. 1/256

Anarríma A constellation. **anar** = sun. S/48

Anarya *Q* 'Sunday'. 3/388

anca *Q* 'jaws'. The name of the Quenya letter *nk.* 3/401

Ancalagon 'Rushing Jaws'. A dragon. 1/70, S/355

Ancalima *S* (Long Light). **an** = long, **cala** = light. 2/418

an(d) 'long'. S/355

andaith 'long mark'. The long-vowel diacritical mark used in Quenya script. 3/400

andave In *Andave laituvalmet!* 3/231

ando *Q* 'gate'. The name for the Quenya letters *d, nd.* Compare *S* **annon.** 3/401

Andor 'The Land of the Gift'. Númenor. **anna** = gift, **dor** = land. S/260

Andram 'The Long Wall'. A cliff in Beleriand. **and** = long, **ram** = wall. S/96

Andrast *S* (Long Shore). The westernmost projection on the north of the Bay of Belfalas. **and** = long, **rast** = shore. o/oo

Androth *S* (Long Foam). The caves in the hills of Mithrim. S/238

Anduin 'The Great River' to the east of the Misty Mountains. **an** = long, **duin** = large river. 1/31

Andúnë *Q* 'West'. R/58

Andúnië *S* (West). The western land of the Faithful in Númenor. **annûn** = west. 3/323

Andúril 'Flame of the West'. The reforged sword of Aragorn. **annûn** = west, **ril** = radiance. 1/290

Anfalas 'Langstrand'. A long coastline in the south of Gondor. **an** = long, **falas** = coast. 3/43

Anfauglir 'Jaws of Thirst'. A name of the wolf Carcharoth. **anca** = jaws, **faug** = gape. S/180

Anfauglith 'The Gasping Dust'. A plain made barren in the Battle of the Sudden Flame. **faug** = gape, **lith** = ash. S/151

ang *S* 'iron'. S/355

anga *Q* 'iron'. S/355

Angainor The chain that bound Morgoth. **anga** = iron. S/51

Angamaite (Ironhand). A corsair of Umbar. **anga** = iron, **maite** = hand. 3/328

Angband 'Iron Prison', 'Hell of Iron'. The dwelling of Morgoth. **ang** = iron, **band** = prison, duress. *Q* **Angamando.** S/206

Angbor (Iron Fist). Lord of Lamedon. **ang** = iron, **bor** = fist, hand. 3/151

Angerthas *S* 'Long Rune-Rows'. The runes, as contrasted with the letters for script writing. **an** = long, **certhas** = runes. 3/404

Angerthas Daeron *S* 'Daeron's Runes'. An early form of runes. 3/401

Angerthas Moria *S* 'Long Rune Rows of Moria'. The later runes devised in Moria. 3/404

Anghabar 'Iron Delvings'. A mine. **ang** = iron. S/201

Anglachel (Iron Star-Flame). The sword, made of meteoric iron, of Thingol, given to Túrin. **ang** = iron, **lach** = leaping flame, **el** = star. S/201

Angmar (Ironhome). The Witch-King's dwelling place at the north end of the Misty Mountains. **ang** = iron, **mar** = home, dwelling. 1/157

angren *S* 'of iron', plural **engrin**. S/356

Angrenost *S* 'Isengard' (Iron Fortress). **angren** = of iron, **ost** = fortress. 2/76

Angrim (Iron-host). A man, father of Gorlim. **ang** = iron, **rim** = host, large number. S/165

Angrist 'Iron-cleaver'. Beren's knife. **ang** = iron, **rist** = cleaver. S/177

Angrod (Iron Champion). A son of Finarfin. **ang** = iron, **aráto** = champion, from **Angaráto.** S/61

Anguirel (Living Star-iron). Eol's sword, made of meteoric iron. **ang** = iron, **el** = star, **guin** = live. S/202

anim *S* 'for myself'. 3/342

Ann-thennath *S* A song mode used in the Lay of Lúthien as chanted by Aragorn. **an** = long, **-ath** = collective plural. 1/205

anna *Q* 'gift'. The name of a Quenya letter for which no English equivalent is given. 3/401

Annael (Star-gift, Elf-gift). The Elf who adopted Tuor. **anna** = gift, **el** = star, Elf. S/238

Annatar 'Lord of Gifts'. A name Sauron gave himself. **anna** = gift, **tar** = lord. S/287

annon *S* 'great door or gate'. S/356

Annon-in-Gelydh *S* 'Gate of the Noldor'. A cavern. **ge-lydh** = *S* form of the *Q* Noldor. S/238

Annúminas *S* (Tower of the West). The royal city of Arnor. **annún** = west, **minas** = tower. 1/257

annún *S* 'west', 'sunset'. 3/401

anor *S* 'sun'. 3/388

Anorien *S* 'Sunlending' (Land of the Sun). Northern Gondor. **anor** = sun, **-ien** = place name suffix. 3/19

anto *Q* 'mouth'. The name of the Quenya letter *nt*. 3/401

Apanónar 'The Afterborn'. An Elvish name for Men. S/103

ar *Q* 'and'. S/356

ar- 'beside', 'outside', 'without'. S/356

ar 'high', 'noble', 'royal'. S/356

Ar *N* prefix of Númenorean royal names, derived from **ar(a)**. S/356

Ar-Adûnakhôr *N* 'Lord of the West'. The nineteenth King of Númenor. **adûn** = west. 3/315

Ar-Feiniel A name of Aredhel, sister of Turgon. S/131

Ar-Gimilzôr *N* The twenty-second King of Númenor. 3/315

Ar-Inziladûn *N* The twenty-third King of Númenor. 3/315

Ar-Pharazôn *N* 'The Golden'. The twenty-fourth and last King of Númenor. 3/316

Ar-Sakalthôr *N* The twenty-first King of Númenor. 3/315

Ar-Zimraphel *N* The royal name of Tar-Míriel, wedded to Ar-Pharazôn. S/269

Ar-Zimrathôn *N* The twentieth King of Númenor. 3/315

ar(a) *S* 'high', 'noble', 'royal'. S/356

Aradan *S* (Noble Man). The Elvish name of Malach, a mortal. S/143

Arador *S* (Lord of the Land). The fifteenth Chieftain of the Dunedain. **dor** = land. 3/318

Araglas *S* (Royal Leaf). The sixth chieftain of the Dunedain. **g-** = augmentive prefix to L, **las** = leaf. 3/318

Aragorn I *S* (Lord of the Tree). The fifth chieftain of the Dunedain. **g-** = augmentive prefix, **orn** = tree. 3/318

Aragorn II *S* (Lord of the Tree). Strider, the King of the reunited Kingdoms of Arnor and Gondor. 3/51

Aragost *S* (Lord of the Fortress). The eighteenth Chieftain of the Dunedain. **g-** = augmentive prefix, **ost** = fortress. 3/318

Arahad I *S* The seventh Chieftain of the Dunedain. 3/318

Arahad II *S* The tenth Chieftain of the Dunedain. 3/318

Arahael *S* The second Chieftain of the Dunedain. 3/318

Araman 'Outside Aman'. A wasteland in the Blessed Realm. S/72

aran *S* 'king', plural **erain.** S/356

Aranarth *S* (King of the Realm). The first Chieftain of the Dunedain. **aran** = king; **arth,** compare **arda,** realm. 3/318

Aranel *S* (King of Elves). A name of Dior. S/188

Aranrúth 'King's Ire'. Thingol's sword. **aran** = king, **rúth** = anger. S/201

Arantar *S* (King of Lords). The sixth King of Arnor. **aran** = king, **tar** = lord. 3/318

Aranuir *S* The third Chieftain of the Dunedain. 3/318

Aranwë (King). An Elf of Gondolin. **aran** = king. S/239

Araphant *S* The fourteenth King of Arthedain. 3/318

Araphor *S* The ninth King of Arthedain. 3/318

Arassuil *S* The eleventh Chieftain of the Dunedain. 3/318

arat 'high', 'noble', 'royal'. S/356

Aratan (Royal Man). A son of Isildur. S/295

Aratar 'The Exalted'. The eight most powerful of the Valar. **arat** = high, **-r** = plural suffix. S/29

Arathorn I *S* (Tree of All Lords). The twelfth Chieftain of the Dunedain. **ar** = royal, **-ath** = collective plural suffix, **orn** = tree. 3/318

Arathorn II *S* (Tree of All Lords). The sixteenth Chieftain of the Dunedain, father of Aragorn II. See **Arathorn I.** 3/318

aráto 'champion', 'eminent man'. S/356

Araval (Lord of Power). The thirteenth King of Arthedain. **ara** = lord, **vala** = power. 3/318

Aravir *S* The fourth Chieftain of the Dunedain. 3/318

Aravorn *S* (Black Lord). The ninth Chieftain of the Dunedain. **ara** = lord, **vorn** = black. 3/318

Araw *S* (Trumpet). A name of Oromë, the Huntsman of the Valar. 3/319

Arciryas (Noble Ship). The brother of King Narmacil II of Gondor. **ar** = noble, high, **ciryas** = ship. 3/330

arda *Q* 'region'. The name of the Quenya letter *rd*.

Arda *Q* 'The Realm'. Earth, the realm of the Valar. S/19

Ard-galen 'The Green Region'. A grassy plain. **arda** = region, **galen** = plural of green. S/106

are *Q* 'sunlight'. The name of the Quenya letter *z*. 3/401

Aredhel 'Noble Elf'. The sister of Turgon. **ar** = noble, **edhel** = Elf. S/60

Argeleb I *S* (Silver King). The seventh King of Arthedain. **ar** = royal, **geleb** from **celeb** = silver. 3/318

Argeleb II *S* (Silver King). The tenth King of Arthedain. See **Argeleb I.** 3/318

Argonath *S* 'The Pair of Royal Stones', 'King Stones'. The pillars marking the border of Gondor on the Anduin. **ar** = royal, king, **gon** = stone, **-ath** = collective plural suffix. R/66

Argonui *S* (Noble commander). The thirteenth Chieftain of the Dunedain. **ar** = noble, royal, **gon** = commander, **-ui** = adjective suffix. As **gon** also means stone, the name could mean Stony King. 3/318

Arien (Maiden of Sunlight). The Maia who sails the Sun.
áre = sunlight, **-ien** = feminine name suffix. S/99

Armenelos (Royal Heaven-fortress). The royal city of
Númenor. **ar** = high, noble, royal, **menel** = heaven,
os = fortress. S/261

Arminas (Royal Tower). An Elf. **ar** = high, noble, royal,
minas = tower. S/212

Arnach *PN* A land in fief to Gondor. 3/125

Arnor 'Land of the King'. **ar** = king, **nor** = land. 1/256

aron *S* (forest). Hypothesized singular of *S* **eryn** =
woods, forest.

Aros *Q* (Foaming). A river in Doriath. **ros** = foam. S/96

Arossiach (Ford of Aros). **iach** = ford. S/121

Artamir (Noble Jewel). The son of Ondoher of Gondor.
arat = high, noble, royal, **mir** = jewel. 3/329

Arthad A companion of Barahir. **ar** = high, noble, royal.
S/155

Arthedain *S* (Realm of Men). A division of Arnor. **arth,**
compare **arda** = realm, **edain** = men. 3/320

Arvedui *S* 'Last King'. The fifteenth and last King of
Arthedain, prophetically named. **ar** = royal, king,
vedui = last. 3/318

Arvegil (Royal Star) *S* The eleventh King of Arthedain.
ar = royal, king, **gil** = star. 3/318

Arveleg I (Mighty King). The eighth King of Arthedain.
ar = royal, king, **veleg,** compare **beleg** = mighty. 3/318

Arveleg II (Mighty King). The twelfth King of Arthedain. See **Arveleg I.** 3/318

Arvernien Lands west of the mouth of Sirion. **ar** = royal,
king, **-ien** = place name suffix. 1/246

Arwen Undomiel (Royal Maiden, Daughter of Twilight).
'Evenstar', daughter of Elrond. **ar** = noble, royal, **wen**

= maiden, **undomë** = twilight, **-iel** = feminine name suffix sometimes translated as 'daughter of'. 3/251

as 'sunlight'. Root word for *áre* and *áze*. S/356

Ascar 'Rushing', 'Impetuous'. A river. S/92

Asëa Aranion (Leaf of Kings). Athelas, a healing herb. **asea,** compare **las** = leaf, **aran** = king. 3/141

Asfaloth *S* Glorfindel's white horse. **loth** = blossom. 1/225

ash *B* 'one'. 1/267

asta *Q* (month). Hypothesized singular of *Q* **astar** = months.

Astaldo 'The Valiant'. A name of Tulkas, a Vala. S/28

astar *Q* 'months'. 3/386

Atalantë 'The Downfallen'. The Quenya equivalent of the Númenorean word **Akallabêth,** the name of sunken Númenor. S/281

atan *Q* 'man'. S/355

Atanatar (Father of Men). The ninth King of Gondor. **atan** = man, **atar** = father. 3/318

Atanatar Alcarin *Q* (Glorious Father of Men). 'The Glorious'. The fifteenth King of Gondor. See **Atanatar. alcarin** = glorious. 3/318

Atanatari *Q* 'Fathers of Men'. S/103

Atani *Q* 'men'. S/355

atar *Q* 'father'. S/356

-ath *S* 'shadow, dimness'. S/359

-ath *S* Collective plural suffix, meaning all of the group to which it is affixed. For example, **giliath** = all the stars. R/66

Aulë The Smith of the Valar. 3/415

aur *S* 'sunlight', 'day'. S/356

aurë 'sunlight', 'day'. S/356

auta *Q* 'is passing'. S/190

Avallonë (Haven near the Valar). City and haven on the Lonely Isle nearest to the Dwellings of the Valar. **a** = to, toward, **vala** = powers, **lonn** = haven, harbor. S/260

avánier *Q* 'have passed away'. Plural verb. R/58

Avari 'The Unwilling', 'The Refusers'. The Dark Elves who never went westward toward the Blessed Realm. S/52

Avathar 'The Shadows'. A desolate land in the Blessed Realm. S/73

Azaghâl *K* The Dwarf-lord of Belegost. S/193

Azanulbizar *K* Dimrill Dale, Nanduhirion. I/296

áze *Q* 'sunlight'. The name of the Quenya letter *z.* 3/401

Azog *O* An Orc-king. 3/354

B

bad 'way'. From **pata.** S/364

bagronk *B* 2/59

bal *S* 'power'. S/365

Balan *S* 'Vala', 'One with Power'. Plural, **Belain.** S/365

Balan *M* Original name of Beör, founder of the eldest House of Men. S/142

Balar A bay and island south of Beleriand. S/57

Balchoth *S* (Host of Power). An evil people in Rhovannion. **bal** = power, **hoth** = enemy host. 3/334

Balrog *S* 'Demon of Might'. Compare *Q* **Valarauko.** Maiar perverted by Morgoth. **bal** = power, **rog** = demon. 1/344

Banakil *H* 'Hobbit', 'Halfling'. **bann** = half, **kil** = diminutive, -ling. 3/416

Banazir *H* 'Sam-wise', 'Half-wise'. **bann** = half. 3/414

band *S* 'prison', 'duress'. S/356

bar *S* 'dwelling'. S/356

Bar-en-Danwedh 'House of Ransom'. A name of the cave of Mîm the Dwarf. S/203

barad *S* 'tower'. Plural **beraid.** S/356

Barad-dûr *S* 'Dark Tower' of Sauron. **dûr** = dark. 1/309

Barad Eithel *S* 'Tower of the Well'. A fortress of the Noldor. **eithel** = well, spring. S/191

Barad Nimras *S* 'White Horn Tower'. The tower of Finrod. **nim** = white, **ras** = horn. S/120

Baragund A companion of Barahir. S/145

Barahir (Tower Lord). Father of Beren. **barad** = tower, **hir** = lord 1/205

Barahir *S* (Towerlord). A grandson of Faramir of Gondor. 1/24

baran *S* 'golden-brown'. 3/416

Baran *S* (Golden Brown). A son of Beör the Old. S/142

Baranduin *S* 'The Brown River'. The Elvish name for the Brandywine River. **baran** = golden-brown, **duin** = large river. 3/416

Baranor (Sun-home). The father of Beregond of Minas Tirith. **bar** = home, dwelling, **anor** = sun. 3/33

Barazinbar *K* Redhorn, Caradhras. 1/296

baruk *K* 'axes'. 3/411

Bauglir 'The Constrainer'. A name of Morgoth. S/104

bel *S* 'powers'. S/365

Belecthor I *S* (Mighty Torrent). The fifteenth Ruling Steward of Gondor. **beleg** = mighty, **thor** = torrent. 3/319

Belecthor II *S* (Mighty Torrent). The twenty-first Ruling Steward of Gondor. See **Belecthor I.** 3/319

beleg *S* 'mighty'. S/356

Beleg *S* 'Mighty'. The archer known as Cúthalion. S/157

Beleg *S* 'Mighty'. The second King of Arthedain. 3/318

Belegaer *S* 'The Great Sea'. Between Middle-earth and the Blessed Realm. **beleg** = mighty, **aer, gaer** = sea. S/37.

Belegorn *S* (Mighty Tree). The fourth Ruling Steward of Gondor. **beleg** = mighty, **orn** = tree. 3/319

Belegost *S* 'Great Fortress'. An ancient Dwarf-city in the Blue Mountains, *K* **Gabilgathol. beleg** = mighty, **ost** = fortress. 3/352

Belegund A companion of Barahir. S/148

Belegûr *S* 'He Who Arises in Might'. *S* form of the name **Melkor** or **Morgoth**. Only used in the form **Belegurth**. S/340

Belegurth *S* 'The Great Death'. See **Belegûr**. S/340

Beleriand 'The Country of Balar'. The land facing the Isle of Balar, later the name of all the lands west to the Blue Mountains. **-iand** = place name suffix. S/120

Belfalas (Coast of the Powers). The bay at the Anduin's mouth and a southern region of Gondor. **bel** = powers, **falas** = coast. 3/442

Belthil 'Divine Radiance'. The image of the White Tree wrought in Gondolin. **bel** = powers, **thil** = shine with white or silver light. S/126

Belthronding (Mighty Hall). The bow of Beleg. **thrond** = hall. S/208

Beör *M* 'Vassal' (of Finrod). Founder of the eldest House of Men. S/142

beraid *S* 'towers'. Singular, **barad.** S/356

Bereg *M* Great-grandson of Beör. S/144

Beregond A guard at Minis Tirith. 3/33

Beren The mortal hero who wedded Lúthien Tinuviel and with her aid recovered a Silmaril. 3/314

bereth *S* 'queen', 'spouse'. R/65

Bergil The young son of Beregond at Minas Tirith. **gil** = star. 3/41

Berhael In *Daur a Berhael, Conin en Annûn!* 3/231

Beruthiel *S* (Daughter of the Queen). A queen in an adage. **bereth** = queen, **-iel** = feminine name suffix sometimes translated as 'daughter of'. 1/325

beth *S* 'word'. 1/320, S/363

Bladorthin An ancient king with whom the Dwarves of the Lonely Mountain traded. May be Old Norse. H/243

Bolg *O, B* An Orc-king of the Misty Mountains, son of Azog. 3/354

bor *S* 'hand', 'fist'. From **paur,** *Q* **quárë** S/357

Bór A chieftain of the Easterlings. S/157

Borgil (Star of the Hand). A red star, probably Aldebaran from its position. **bor** = hand, **gil** = star 1/91

Borlach *S* (Flaming Hand). A son of Bór of the Easterlings. **bor** = hand, **lach** = leaping flame. This may be a name in a mortal tongue and untranslatable. S/157

Borlad *S* (Plain of the Hand). A son of Bór of the Easterlings. **bor** = hand, **lad** a plain. See note on **Borlach.** S/157

Boromir (Jeweled Hand). The great-grandfather of Beren. **bor** = hand, **mir** = jewel. S/148

Boromir (Jeweled Hand). The eleventh Ruling Steward of Gondor. See above. 3/319

Boromir (Jeweled Hand). One of the Fellowship of the Ring. See above. 1/253

Boron (Great Hand). The great-great-grandfather of Beren. **bor** = hand, **-on** = augmentive suffix. This may be an untranslatable mortal name. S/148

Borthand A son of Bór of the Easterlings. S/157

bragol 'sudden'. S/356

Bralda-hîm *H* 'Heady Ale'. The Brandywine River. 3/416

Braldagamba *H* 'Brandy-buck'. 3/416

Branda-nin *H* 'Border-water'. The Brandywine River. 3/416

Brandagamba *H* 'March-buck' (**march** meaning border). Brandybuck. 3/416

Brandir A ruler of the People of Haleth. S/216

bre A syllable associated with trees, perhaps meaning **branch,** in Bregalad, Nimbrethil, and Fimbrethil.

Bregalad *S* Quickbeam, the rowan-ent. **galad** = tree. 2/86

Bregolas A man. **las** = leaf. S/148

Bregor A man, father of Barahir and Bregolas. S/148

brethil 'silver birch'. **thil** = shine with white or silver light. S/356

Brethil 'Silver Birch'. The forest where the People of Haleth lived. S/120

Brilthor 'Glittering Torrent'. One of the seven rivers of Ossiriand. **ril** = brilliance, **thor** = torrent. S/123

brith 'gravel'. S/356

Brithiach (Gravel Ford). A ford of the Sirion. **brith** = gravel, **iach** = ford. S/131

Brithombar A northern harbor of Beleriand. **brith** = gravel. S/58

Brithon (Gravel). The river which led down to Brithombar. **brith** = gravel, **-on** = augmentive suffix. S/58

Brodda An Easterling. S/198

Bruinen 'Loudwater'. **nen** = water. 1/212

bûbhosh *O* or *B.* 2/48

Bundushathur *K* Fanuidhol, Cloudyhead. 1/296

burz *B* (dark). See **Lugburz, burzum-ishi.**

burzum-ishi *B* 'in the darkness'. 1/267

C

Cabed-en-Aras A gorge on the river Teiglin. S/221

Cabed Naeramarth 'Leap of Dreadful Doom'. The name

of Cabed-en-Aras after Nienor there jumped to her death. **amarth** = doom. S/224

Cair Andros 'Ship of Long Foam'. An island in the Anduin. **cair** from **cir** = ship, **and** = long, **ros** = foam. 3/335

caita *Q* 'lies'. Verb. R/62

cal 'shine'. The root word for **cala** and **galad** = light, **calma** = lamp, and **calen, galen** = green, which is literally 'bright'. S/360

Cala-cirya *Q* 'Light Cleft'. The ravine in the Blessed Realm lit by the Two Trees. **cala** = light, **cir** = cleft. R/62

Calacirian *Q* 'Light Cleft'. See **Cala-cirya. -ian** = place name suffix. R/59

Calaciriande *Q* 'Light Cleft'. See **Cala-cirya. -iande** = place name suffix. R/59

Calaciryo *Q* 'Light-Cleft's'. See **Cala-cirya. -o** = possessive suffix. R/59

Calaquendi *Q* 'Elves of Light'. The High Elves, who had lived in the Blessed Realm in the light of the Two Trees. **cala** = light, **quendi** = elves, literally, 'speakers'. S/53

Calembel (Divine Green). A hill city in southern Gondor. **calem** from **calen** = green, **bel** = powers, divine. 3/63

calen *S* 'green'. Literally 'bright'. S/356

Calenardhon 'The Green Province'. A former name of Rohan. **calen** = green, **arda** = region. 2/287

Calenhad A beacon hill. **calen** = green. 3/19

Calimehtar *Q* (Swordsman of Light). The twenty-ninth King of Gondor. **cala** = light, **mehtar** = swordsman. 3/319

Calimmacil *Q* (Sword of Light). The son of Arciryas of Gondor. **cala** = light, **megil** = sword. 3/330

calma *Q* 'lamp'. The name of the Quenya letter *k.* 3/401

calma-téma *Q* 'lamp-series'. The K-series of Tengwar letters. **calma** = lamp, **téma** = series. 3/401

Calmacil *Q* (Bright Sword). The seventeenth King of Gondor. **cal** = shine, **megil** = sword. 3/318

cam *S* 'hand'. The cupped hand, holding or receiving. S/356

Camlost *S* 'Empty-handed'. A name of Beren. **cam** = hand. S/184

carach *S* 'jaws', 'fangs'. S/357

Carach Angren *S* 'Isenmouthe'. In Mordor. **carach** = jaws, **angren** = of iron. 3/190

Caradhras *S* 'Redhorn'. From **caran** = red, **ras** = horn. 1/296

carag 'fang'. S/357

Caragdûr (Dark Fang). A precipice on the hill of Gondolin. **carag** = fang, **dûr** = dark. S/138

carack *S* 'fang'. S/357

caran *S* 'red'. S/357

Caran-rass 'Redhorn'. A form of the name **Caradhras**. **caran** = red, **ras** = horn. 3/391

Caranthir (Red River). A son of Fëanor. **caran** = red, **sir** = river. S/60

Caras Galadon *Sv.* The city in Lórien. **galad** = light, **-on** = augmentive suffix. **Caras** may be a form of **coron** = mound. 1/368

carca *Q* 'fang'. S/357

carch *S* 'fang'. S/357

Carcharoth *S* 'The Red Maw'. The wolf of Angband. **caran** = red, **carch** = fang. S/180

Carchost *S* 'Fang Fort'. One of the Towers of the Teeth in Mordor. **carch** = fang, **ost** = fortress. 3/176

Cardolan A division of Arnor. **caran** = red, **dol** = head. 3/320

Carn Dûm (Red Fort). The Witch-King's fortress in Angmar. **caran** = red, **Dûm** compare Khazad-dûm 'The Mansions of the Dwarves'. 1/154

carnë *Q* 'red'. S/357

Carnemírië *Q* 'red-jeweled'. A rowan tree. **carne** = red, **mir** = jewel. 2/87

Carnen 'Redwater'. A river flowing from the Iron Mountains. **caran** = red, **nen** = water. 3/353

Carnil (Red Point). A red star. **caran** = red, **nil** from **dil** = point. S/48

Castamir The usurper of the throne of Gondor. **mir** = jewel. 3/319

ceber *S* 'stake'. S/364

cebir *S* 'stakes'. S/364

cel 'go away', 'flow away', 'flow down'. S/360

Celduin *S* 'River Running'. The river that flows from the Long Lake. **cel** = flow, **duin** = large river. 3/353

celeb *S* 'silver'. 3/391

Celebdil *S* 'Silvertine'. **celeb** = silver, **dil** = point. 1/296

Celeborn *S* 'Tree of Silver'. The descendant of the White Tree on the Lonely Isle. **celeb** = silver, **orn** = tree. S/59

Celeborn *S* 'Tree of Silver'. The Elven Lord of Lórien. See above. 1/268

Celebrant *S* 'Silver Course', 'Silverlode'. The river running from Mirrormere through Lórien. **celeb** = silver, **rant** = course. 1/355

Celebrian *S* (Silver Maiden). The daughter of Galadriel, mother of Arwen, wedded to Elrond. **celeb** = silver, **-ian** = feminine name suffix. 1/391

Celebrimbor *S* 'Hand of Silver', 'Silver Fist'. Elven master-wright in Eregion who wrought the Three Elven Rings. **celebrin** = silverlike, **bor** = hand, fist. 1/255

celebrin *S* 'like silver in hue or worth'. S/357

Celebrindal *S* 'Silverfoot'. The daughter of Turgon, wedded to Tuor. **celebrin** = silverlike, **dal** = foot. 3/314

Celebrindor *S* (Silver Lord). The fifth King of Arthedain. **celebrin** = silverlike, **dor** from **tar** = high, lord. 3/318

Celebros 'Silver Foam', 'Silver Rain'. A stream with a waterfall in Brethil. **celeb** = silver, **ros** = foam. S/220

Celegorm A son of Fëanor. **celeb** = silver. S/60

Celepharn *S.* The fourth King of Arthedain. **celeb** = silver. 3/318

Celon 'Stream Flowing Down from the Heights'. A river tributary to the Aros. **cel** = flow down, **-on** = augmentive suffix. S/96

Celos *S* (Flowing Snow). A river in southern Gondor. **cel** = flow down, **los** = snow-white. 3/151

Cemendur (Lover of the Earth). The third King of Gondor. **kemen** = earth, **-dur** = lover of, devoted to. 3/318

cerin 'mound'. S/357

Cerin Amroth *Sv* (Amroth's Mound). The hill where Amroth lived in Lórien. **cerin** = mound. 1/366

Cermië *Q* The month corresponding to July. *S* **Cerveth**. 3/388

certa *Q* (rune). The hypothesized singular form of **certar** = runes.

Certar *Q* 'Runes'. The angular letters used most for incised inscriptions. 3/401

Certhas *S* 'Runes'. See **Certar**. 3/401

Cerveth *S* The month corresponding with July. *Q* **Cermië**. 3/388

cham 'hand'. S/356

chil 'heir', as in **Eluchil**. S/327

cir 'cleave', 'cut'. Compare **Cirth** = 'Runes', **Certhas** = 'Runes', **Cirith** = 'Pass', **Calacirian** = 'Light Cleft', S/363

cir 'ship'. Because it cleaves or cuts through the waves. S/360

Cirdan *S* 'Shipwright'. Elven Lord of the Gray Havens. **cir** = ship, **dan** = wright. 1/253

Ciril (Brilliant Cleft, Cleft of the Star). A river in southern Gondor. **cir** = cut, cleft, **ril** = brilliant, **il** = star. 3/63

Cirion (Lord of Ships). The twelfth Ruling Steward of Gondor. **cir** = ship, **-ion** = masculine name suffix sometimes translated as 'lord of'. 2/287

cirith (cleft, pass). See following entries.

Cirith Gorgor 'Haunted Pass'. The pass into Mordor. **cirith** = cleft, **gorgor** = horror. 1/390

Cirith Ninniach 'Rainbow Cleft'. A cavern. **cirith** = cleft, **ninniach** seems to mean literally 'wet ford' but still may translate as 'rainbow'. S/238

Cirith Thoronath 'Eagles' Cleft'. A high pass. **cirith** = cleft, **thoron** = eagle, **-ath** = collective plural suffix. S/243

Cirith Ungol 'Spider's Pass'. The pass near Shelob's Lair. **cirith** = cleft, **ungol** = spider. 2/252

Cirth 'Runes'. The angular letters used for most incised inscriptions. 3/395

ciryà 'sharp-prowed ship'. S/360

Ciryaher Hyarmendacil *Q* (Ship Lord). 'South Victor'. The fourteenth King of Gondor, victorious over the Corsairs of Umbar. **cirya** = ship, **her** = lord, **hyarmen** = south, **dacil** = victor. 3/318

Ciryandil *Q* (Ship-lover). The thirteenth King of Gondor. **cirya** = ship, **-dil** = friend, lover. 3/318

Ciryon (Great Ship). A son of Isildur. **cir** = ship, **-on** = augmentive suffix. S/295

coi 'life'. S/357

coimas *Q* 'life bread'. *S* **lembas** = waybread from **lennbas** = journey bread. S/357

coirë *Q* 'stirring'. *S* **echuir**. The pre-spring season in the Elvish six-season year. 3/386

collo 'cloak'. S/365

cor (ring). See the following entries.

coranor *S* 'sun-round'. The solar year. **cor** = ring, **anor** = sun. 3/385

cormacolindor (ringbearers). **cor** = ring. 3/231

Cormallen *S* 'Golden Circle'. Field where the destruction of the One Ring was celebrated. **cor** = ring, **mal** = gold. The field was named for the red-gold flowering **culumalda** trees growing there. S/361, 3/235

Cormarë 'Ringday'. The day of celebration of the destruction of the One Ring. **cor** = ring, **arë** = sunlight, day. 3/390

corol 'mound'. S/357

Corollaire 'The Green Mound' in the Blessed Realm where the Two Trees grew. **corol** = mound, **laire** = summer, may literally mean 'green'. S/38

coron 'mound'. S/357

Coron Oiolaire 'The Mound of Eversummer'. A name for **Corollaire**. S/357

craban Hypothesized singular for **crebain** = crows.

Crissaegrim (Cleaving Points). The mountains south of Gondolin. **cris** = cleave, **ae** = point, **rim** = host, large number. S/121

crist 'cleave'. From **kir**. S/360

crebain *S* crows. Compare English *raven*. 1/298

cú 'bow'. S/357

cuio *S* (live). Imperative verb. 3/231

cuivië 'awakening'. S/357

Cuiviénen *Q* 'Water of Awakening'. The lake by which the Elves first awoke. *S* **Nen Echui. cuivië** = awakening, **nen** = water. S/48

cul 'golden-red'. S/357

culumalda (red gold). The trees for which the Field of Cormallen was named. **cul** = golden red, **mal** = gold. S/361

Culurien (Golden Maiden). A name for the Golden Tree. **cul** = golden-red, **-ien** = maiden. S/38

curu 'skill'. S/357

Curufin (Skilled One of [Beautiful] Hair). A son of Fëanor. **curu** = skill, **fin** = hair. S/60

Curufinwë (Skilled One of [Beautiful] Hair). A name of Fëanor. See above. S/63

Curunir 'The One of Cunning Devices', 'Man of Skill'. Elvish name of Saruman. **curu** = skill. 3/365

Cúthalion 'Strongbow'. A name of Beleg the Archer. **cú** = bow, **thalion** = strong, steadfast. S/201

D

dacil *Q* 'victor'. From **ndak** = battle. S/357

dae 'shadow'. S/357

Dearon The minstrel and loremaster of King Thingol, inventor of the rune system Angerthas Daeron. **dae** = shadow. 3/397

dagnir 'bane'. S/357

Dagnir 'Bane'. A companion of Barahir. S/155

Dagnir Glaurunga 'Glaurung's Bane'. A title of Turin. S/148

dagor 'battle'. S/357

Dagor Aglareb 'The Glorious Battle'. A battle in the Wars of Beleriand. **dagor** = battle, **aglareb** = glorious. S/155

Dagor Bragollach 'The Battle of Sudden Flame'. A battle in the Wars of Beleriand. **dagor** = battle, **bragol** = sudden, **lach** = leaping flame. S/151

Dagor-nuin-Gilliath 'The Battle under the Stars'. A battle of the Wars of Beleriand. **dagor** = battle, **nuin** = under, **gilliath** = the star-host. S/106

Dagorlad (The Battle Plain). The barren plain north of the gates of Mordor. **dagor** = battle, **lad** = plain. 2/232

Dairuin A companion of Barahir. **ruin** = red flame. S/155

dal 'foot'. S/357

Damrod One of Faramir's rangers in Ithilien. **rod** = power. 2/267

dan (take). 1/312

dan (wright). Plural, **dain.** Probably from **adan** = man. See **Cirdan** = Shipwright, **Celerdain** = Lampwrights, **Mirdain** = Jewelwrights.

daro (halt). An imperative verb. 1/356

daur In *Daur a Berhael, Conin en Annun!* 3/231

del 'horror'. S/357

Deldúwath 'Horror of Night Shadow'. A name for Dorthonion. **del** = horror, **dú** = night, **wath** = shadow. S/155

deloth 'abhorrence'. S/357

Denethor (Water Torrent). A leader of the Nandorian Elves. **den** from **nen** = water, **thor** = torrent. S/54

Denethor I (Water Torrent). The tenth Ruling Steward of Gondor. 3/319

Denethor II (Water Torrent). The twenty-sixth and last Ruling Steward of Gondor, father of Boromir and Faramir. 3/319

Derufin A son of Duinhir of Morthond. **fin** = hair. 3/43

Dervorin A son of the lord of Ringlo Vale. 3/43

dhol 'head'. From **dol.** S/357

di'nguruthos *S* 'beneath death-horror'. Compare **gurth** = death. R/64

-dil 'friend', 'lover of', 'devoted to'. Suffix of several personal names. S/362

dil 'point', 'horn'. S/365

dim 'sad', 'gloomy'. S/356

Dimbar (Gloomy Home). The land between the rivers Sirion and Mindeb. **dim** = sad, gloomy, **bar** = home, dwelling. S/121

Dimrost 'The Rainy Stair'. The falls of the Celebros. S/220

din 'sparkle'. S/365

dîn 'silent'. S/357

Dior The son of Lúthien and Beren, father of Elwing. 1/206

dir (gaze, watch). Compare **tir** = watch.

Dírhael The maternal grandfather of Aragorn. 3/337

diriel *S* 'gazing'. R/64

díriel *S* 'gaze'. R/64

dol 'head'. S/357

Dol Amroth (Amroth's Hill). Prince Imrahil's dwelling place, named for the Elven King Amroth who was lost at sea nearby. **dol** = head, often applied to hills. 3/22

Dol Baran (Golden Brown Head). The southernmost hill of the Misty Mountains. **dol** = head, **baran** = golden-brown. 2/194

Dol Guldûr 'Hill of Sorcery'. Sauron the Necromancer's tower in Mirkwood. **dol** = head, often applied to hills, **gul** = sorcery, **dûr** = dark. 1/263

Dolmed 'Wet Head'. One of the Blue Mountains. **dol** = head, **med** = wet. S/91

dolen *S* 'hidden'. S/359

dōmē *S* 'dusk'. S/358

don (lofty). See **Mindon** = Lofty Tower.

dor *S* 'land'. S/357

dor 'lord'. S/365

Dor Caranthir 'Land of Caranthir'. A name for Thargelion. S/124

Dor Cúarthol 'Land of Bow and Helm'. The land around Amon Rûdh. **dor** = land, **cú** = bow, **ar** = and, **thol** = helm. S/205

Dor Daedeloth 'Land of the Shadow of Horror'. The land of Morgoth. **dor** = land, **dae** = shadow, **deloth** = abhorrence. S/107

Dor Dínen 'The Silent Land'. A desolate land. **dor** = land, **dínen** = silent. S/121

Dor-en-Ernil (Land of the Prince). A land in Gondor between Belfalas and Lebennin. **dor** = land, **en** = of, **Ernil** = prince. 3/00

Dor Firn-i-Guinar 'Land of the Dead that Live'. The land where Beren and Lúthien dwelt after their return from death. **dor** = land, **firn** = dead, **i** = the, that, **guinar** = live. **Guinar** is a plural verb of the same root as **cuivië** = live. S/188

Dor-lómin (Land of Echos). A land in the south of Hithlum. **dor** = land, **lóm** = echo. S/89

Dor-nu-Fauglith 'Land under Choking Ash'. A name for Anfauglith. **dor** = land, **nu** = under, **faug** = gape, **lith** = ash. S/153

Doriath 'Land of the Fence'. The land of Melian and Thingol. **dor** = land, **iâth** = fence, referring to the protective magic Girdle of Melian. 1/256, S/97

Dorlas (Lord of Leaf). A man of the Haladin. **dor** from **tar** = lord, **las** = leaf. S/224

Dorthonion 'Land of Pines'. A forested highland north of Doriath. **dor** = land, **thon** = pine tree, **-ion** = place name suffix. 2/72

Dorwinion (Wineland). The land in the south where wine was made for Thranduil. This may be a part-English word in the style of Elvish place names. **dor** = land, **-ion** = place-name suffix. H/190

draug 'wolf'. S/358

Draugluin (Blue Wolf). A werewolf. **draug** = wolf, **luin** = blue. S/174

Drengist A long firth. S/54

dru (Wose). See **Druadan Forest,** where the Woses lived, and **Druwaith Iaur** 'Old Púkel-land'.

Druadan *S* (Wose-man). The forest of the Woses. 3/104

Druwaith Iaur 'Old Púkel Land'. 0/00

du *S* 'night', 'dimness'. S/358

dui *S* 'flow [in volume]'. C/179

Duilin (River Song). A son of Duinhir of Morthond. **duin** = river, **lin** = song. 3/43

Duilwen (Riversheen). A firth. **duil** from **duin** = large river, **wen** = sheen. S/123

duin *S* 'large river'. 3/416

duinē *S* 'large river'. C/179

Duinhir *S* (Riverlord). The Lord of Morthond. **duin** = large river, **hir** = lord. 3/43

dûn *S* 'west'. 3/401

dun *S* 'valley'. S/365

Dúnadan *S* 'Man of the West'. A descendant of the Númenoreans, Aragorn's name in Rivendell. **dûn** = west, **adan** = man. 1/222

Dúnedain *S* 'Men of the West'. **dûn** = west, **edain** = men. 3/48

dûr 'dark'. S/358

dur 'friend', 'lover of', 'devotion', 'devoted to'. A personal name suffix. S/362

durbatulûk *B* 'to rule them all'. 1/267

Durthang (Dark Oppression). A castle in northern Mordor. **dûr** = dark, **thang** = oppression. 3/205

E

Eä 'It Is', 'Let It Be'. The World, meaning the entire material universe, not only Earth, from the word spoken by Iluvatar (Eru) at the beginning of the universe. S/20

eär *Q* 'sea'. R/65

Eärello *Q* (from the Sea). **eär** = sea, **-ello** = from, of. 3/245

Eärendil *Q* 'Lover of the Sea'. The mariner who bears the Silmaril as the Morning Star. Old English **Earendel** 'first light', 'first dawn' was the name of the Morning Star and had religious significance. **eär** = sea, **-dil** = lover of. 1/206

Eärendur *Q* (Lover of the Sea). A Lord of Andunië in Númenor. **eär** = sea, **dur** = lover of. S/268

Eärendur *Q* (Lover of the Sea). The eleventh and last King of Arnor. 3/318

Eärenya *Q* 'Seaday'. 3/388

Eärnil I *Q* (Lover of the Sea). The twelfth King of Gondor. **eär** = sea, **nil** = lover of. 3/318

Eärnil II *Q* (Lover of the Sea). The thirty-first King of Gondor. 3/318

Eärnur *Q* (Lover of the Sea). The thirty-second and last King of Gondor. **eär** = sea, **-nur** = lover of. 3/319

Eärrámë *Q* 'Sea Wing'. Tuor's ship. **eär** = sea, **rama** = wing. S/245

Eärwen *Q* (Seamaiden). The daughter of Thingol's brother. **eär** = sea, **wen** = maiden. S/60

echant *S* (made). 1/319

echor 'encircling wall'. Compare **cor** = ring, circle. S/358

Echoriath 'The Encircling Mountains' around Gondolin. **echor** = encircling wall, **iâth** = fence. S/115

echuir *S* 'stirring'. The season before spring in the Elvish six-season year. *Q* **coirë.** 3/386

Ecthelion An Elf Lord of Gondolin. S/107

Ecthelion I The seventeenth Ruling Steward of Gondor. 3/319

Ecthelion II The twenty-fifth Ruling Steward of Gondor, father of Denethor II. 3/319

Edain *S* 'men'. Particularly the first three houses of men to come into Beleriand. Singular **adan.** 3/314

edhel *S* 'elf'. S/358

edhellen *S* (of the elves). 1/320

Edhellond (Elf Haven). A harbor near Dol Amroth. 0/00

edhil *S* 'elves'. S/358

Edrahil An Elf of Nargothrond. **hil** = follower, heir. S/170

edraith *S* In *Naur an edraith ammen!* 1/304

edro *S* 'open'. An imperative verb. 1/320

Egalmoth The eighteenth Ruling Steward of Gondor. **moth** = dusk. 3/319

Egladil (Forsaken Point). The Angle of Lorien. **egla** = forsaken, **dil** = point. 1/316

Eglador (Land of the Forsaken). A former name of Doriath as land of the Eglath. **egla** = forsaken, **dor** = land. S/97

Eglamar (Home of the Forsaken). T/77

Eglarest (Forsaken Shore). A haven in the south of Beleriand. **egla** = forsaken, **rast** = shore. S/58

Eglath 'The Forsaken People'. A name of the Telerin Elves when they remained in Beleriand searching for Thingol. **egla** = forsaken, **-ath** = collective plural suffix. S/58

eglerio *S* (glorify). An imperative verb. 3/231

ehtelë *Q* 'spring', 'well'. Compare **kel** = flow away. S/360

Eilenach *PN* A beacon hill. 3/19

Eilinel The wife of Gorlim. **el** = star. S/162

eithel *S* 'spring, well'. Compare **kel** = flow away. S/358

Eithel Ivren 'Ivren's Well'. The source of the river Narog. **eithel** = spring, well. S/209

Eithel Sirion 'Sirion's Well'. The source of the river Sirion. **eithel** = spring, well. S/107

Ekkaia (The Outer Sea) which encircled the world. **et** = out, **gaer** = sea. S/37

el *Q* 'star'. R/65

êl *S* 'star'. R/65

Elbereth *S* 'Star Queen'. A title of the Vala Varda. **el** = star, **bereth** = queen. R/64

Elanor *S* 'Sunstar'. A yellow, star-shaped flower growing in Lórien, after which Samwise's first daughter was named. **el** = star, **anor** = sun. 1/365

elda 'of the stars'. S/358

Eldacar (Red Elf). The fourth King of Arnor. **elda** = elf, **caran** = red. 3/318

Eldalië 'The Elven Folk'. S/22

Eldamar *Q* 'Elvenhome'. **elda** = elf, **mar** = home. 1/247

Eldar *Q* 'Elves', 'People of the Stars'. 1/235

Eldarion (Son of Elves). The heir of Aragorn Elessar. **eldar** = elves, **-ion** = masculine name suffix sometimes translated as 'son of'. 3/343

ele 'behold'. Said when the Elves first saw the stars. S/358

Eledh *S* 'Elf'. S/358

Eledwen *S* 'Elfsheen'. The mother of Túrin. **eledh** = elf, **wen** = sheen. S/148

Elemmírë *Q* (Star Jewel). A star. **elen** = star, **mírë** = jewel. S/48

Elemmírë *Q* (Star Jewel). An Elf of the Vanyar. S/76

elen 'star'. 1/90

Elen-tari *Q* 'Star Queen'. A title of the Vala Varda. **elen** = star, **tari** = queen. R/58

elena 'of the stars'. S/358

elenath *S* 'star-host'. **elen** = star, **-ath** = collective plural suffix. R/65

Elende A name of Elvenhome. **elen** = star. S/61

Elendil 'Elf-friend', 'Star-lover'. The leader of the Faithful from Númenor, first King of Arnor and Gondor. **elen** = star, **dil** = friend, lover of. 1/246

Elendili 'Elf-friends'. The Faithful Númenoreans. S/266

Elendilmir 'Star of Elendil'. A jewel, the heirloom of the House of Elendil. **mir** = jewel. 3/323

Elendur (Star-lover). A son of Isildur. **elen** = star, **dur** = lover of. S/295

Elendur (Star-lover). The tenth King of Arnor. 3/319

eleni *Q* 'stars'. Singular **elen** R/65

Elenion (Star). In *Aiya Earendil Elenion Ancalima!* **elen** = star, **-ion** = masculine name suffix. 2/329

Elenna 'Starwards'. A name of Númenor. **elen** = star. S/261

Elenwë (Star). The wife of Turgon. **elen** = star. S/90

Elenya *Q* 'Starsday'. **elen** = star. 3/388

Elerrína 'Crowned with Stars'. A name of the highest peak in the Blessed Realm, where Varda and Manwe dwelt. S/37

Elessar *Q* 'Elfstone'. The royal name of Aragorn. **el** = Elf, **sarn** = small stone. 3/319

elin *S* 'stars'. R/65

Elladan (Man of the Elves, Man of the Stars). A son of Elrond. **el** = elf, star, **adan** = man. 1/239

-ello *Q* (from, of). See **Sindanoriello** = from the Gray Country, and **Earello** = from the Sea

Elostirion (Star Watch Tower). The tallest tower of the Tower Hills, where the Palantir was kept. **el** = star, **ost** = fortress, **tir** = watch, **-ion** = place name suffix. S/292

Elrohir (Star Horse Lord). A son of Elrond. **el** = star, **roh** = horse, **hir** = lord. 1/239

Elrond 'Star Dome'. A son of Eärendil, greatest of the Wise. **el** = star, **rond** = dome. 1/182

Elros Tar-Minyatur 'Star Foam' (Lord First Master). A son of Eärendil, first King of Númenor. **el** = star, **ros** = foam, **tar** = high, noble, **minya** = first, **tur** = master. 3/315

Elu *S* (Star). *Q* **Elwë**. The name of King Thingol. S/56

Eluchíl *S* 'Heir of Elu'. A name of Dior, Thingol's heir. **chíl** from **híl** = heir, follower. S/188

Eluréd *S* 'Heir of Elu'. The eldest son of Dior. S/234

Elurín *S* 'Remembrance of Elu'. A son of Dior. S/234

Elwë Singollo *Q* (Star) 'Graymantle'. *S* **Elu Thingol**, Lord of Doriath. **sin(d)** = gray, **gollo** = cloak. S/52

Elwing 'Star Spray'. The mother of Elrond and Elros, wedded to Eärendil, named for the waterfall at her birthplace. **el** = star, **wing, ving** = spray. 1/206

elye *Q* 'even thou'. R/59

Emeldir The mother of Beren. **mel** = love. S/155

emyn *S* 'hills'. Singular **amon** 3/393

Emyn Arnen *S* (Royal Water Hills). The hills south of

Ithilien, Faramir's Princedom. **emyn** = hills, **ar** = royal, **nen** = water. 3/22

Emyn Beraid *S* 'Tower Hills' near the Gray Havens. **emyn** = hills, **beraid** = towers. 3/322

Emyn Muil *S* The bleak hills north of Rauros. **emyn** = hills. 1/390

en (of the). Used in many place names such as **Dor-en-Ernil** = Land of the Prince.

Ennorath *S* 'Middle-earth'. **ened** = middle, **dor** = land, **-ath** = collective plural suffix. R/64

Enderi 'Middle Days'. The three midsummer holidays. **ened** = middle, **arë** = day, sunlight. 3/386

Endor 'Middle Land'. Middle Earth. **ened** = middle, **dor** = land. S/89

Endóre 'Middle Earth'. **ened** = middle, **dor** = land. 3/490

Endorenna 'Middle Earth'. **ened** = middle, **dor** = land. 3/245

ened 'middle'. S/259

Enedwaith 'Middle-folk'. The land between the Isen and the Gwathlo. **ened** = middle, **waith** = people. 1/00

engrin *S* 'of iron' plural. S/356

Engwar 'The Sickly'. An Elvish name for Men. S/103

Ennor 'Middle Earth'. **ened** = middle, **nor** = land. 3/393

ennyn *S* 'gates', 'doors'. Singular **annon**. 1/319

enquantuva *Q* 'refill-will'. **uva** = will. R/58

enquie *Q* 'week'. Plural **enquier**. 3/385

enquier *Q* 'weeks'. Singular **enquie**. 3/385

entuluva *Q* 'shall come again'. S/195

Enyd *S* 'Ents'. Singular **Onod**. 3/408

Eöl The Dark Elf. S/92

Eönwë A Maia, the herald of Manwë. S/30

ephel *S* 'outer fence'. **et** = out, **pel** = fence, border. 3/392

Ephel Brandir 'The Encircling Fence of Brandir'. A stronghold of the men of Brethil. S/216

Ephel Duath 'Mountains of Shadow'. The mountains on the west side of Mordor. **ephel** = outer fence, **dú** = dimness, **wath** = shadow plural suffix. 2/244

er 'one', 'alone'. S/358

Eradan (Lonely Man). The second Ruling Steward of Gondor. **er** = alone, **adan** = man. 3/319

erain *S* 'kings'. Singular **aran.** S/356

Erchamion 'One Handed'. A name of Beren after he lost his hand to the wolf of Angband. **er** = one, **cam** = hand, **-ion** = masculine name suffix. S/183

ereb 'lonely'. S/358

Erebor 'The Lonely Mountain'. **ereb** = lonely, **oro(d)** = mountain. 1/21

Erech *PN* The place where Elendil had set up the stone at which the Dead swore fealty to Aragorn. 3/55

ered *S* (mountains). Singular **orod.** See following entries.

Ered Engrin 'The Iron Mountains' in the far north. **engrin** = of iron. S/109

Ered Gorgoroth 'The Mountains of Terror' in southern Dorthonion. **gorgor** = horror. S/81

Ered Lindon (Mountains of Lofty Song) (Mountains of the Lofty Wave). A name of the Blue Mountains. **lin** = song, wave, **don** = lofty. S/123

Ered Lithui *S* 'Ashen Mountains'. The mountains on the northern border of Mordor. **lith** = ash, **-ui** = adjective suffix. 2/244

Ered Lómin *S* 'The Echoing Mountains' west of Hithlum. **lóm** = echo. S/106

Ered Luin *S* 'The Blue Mountains'. The mountain range in Lindon. **luin** = blue. 1/00

Ered Mithrin *S* 'The Gray Mountains' north of Mirkwood. **mith** = gray. 1/oo

Ered Nimrais *S* 'White Horn Mountains' forming the border between Rohan and Gondor. **nim** = white, **rais** = horns. 1/271

Ered Wethrin 'Mountains of Shadow', 'The Shadowy Mountains'. A major mountain range dividing Beleriand. **weth** = shadow. S/107

ereg 'thorn', 'holly'. S/358

Eregion 'Land of Holly'. Hollin, an Elven land west of Moria. **ereg** = holly, **-ion** = place name suffix. 1/56

erein *S* 'kings'. Singular **aran**. S/356

Ereinion 'Scion of Kings'. A name of Gil-galad. **erein** = kings, **-ion** = a masculine name suffix sometimes translated as 'son of'. S/154

Erelas (Lone Leaf). A beacon hill. **er** = alone, **las** = leaf. 3/19

Erellont A companion of Eärendil. S/248

Eresseä 'The Lonely Isle' on which the Elves were conveyed to the Blessed Realm. **er** = alone. R/61

Erestor An Elven Lord of Elrond's household. **er** = one. 1/253

Eriador The west lands. **er** = one, **dor** = land. 1/13

Erin Vorn *S* (Black Woods). A forest in Minhiriath. **erin** from **eryn** = woods, **vorn** = black. o/oo

Eriol 'One who dreams alone'. A character in an early form of the Silmarillion. **er** = alone. T/90

ernil 'prince'. 3/41

Eru 'The One', 'He That Is Alone'. Iluvatar, the All-Father. **er** = one, alone. S/15

Erui (Lone). A river in Gondor tributary to the Anduin. **er** = alone, **-ui** = adjective suffix. 3/151

Erusen 'The Children of God'. Elves and Men. **Eru** = The One. R/66

eryn (woods). 3/375

Eryn Lasgallen 'Greenwood the Great' (Wood of Green-leaves). The name of Mirkwood after its cleansing. **eryn** = woods, **las** = leaf, **galen** = green. 3/375

esgal 'screen', 'hiding'. S/358

Esgalduin 'River under Veil'. The enchanted river in Doriath. **esgal** = screen, **duin** = large river. 1/206

Esgaroth (Hiding Foam). Laketown below the Lonely Mountain. **esgal** = hiding, **roth** from **ros** = foam. 1/38

essë *Q* 'name'. The alternative name for the Quenya letter *s.* 3/401

-esse *Q* (in). See **Lóriendesse.**

Estë 'Rest'. A queen of the Valar. S/25

Estel 'Hope'. Aragorn's name as a youth in Rivendell. 3/338

Estolad 'The Encampment'. A land where Men dwelt after crossing the Blue Mountains. S/142

et *Q* (out). 3/245

et-kele 'issue of water', 'a spring'. S/360

Ethir Anduin *S* (Outflow of the Anduin). **et** = out, **thir** from **sir** = flow. 1/416

Ethring (Cold Spring). A town on a river-crossing in Gondor. **et** = out, **ring** = cold. 3/00

ethuil *S* 'spring'. The season. *Q* **tuilë.** 3/386

-eva *Q* (of). See **miruvoreva** = nectar of.

Ezellohar The green mound where the Two Trees grew. S/38

F

Faelivren A name of Finduilas. S/210

falas 'coast', 'shore', 'line of surf'. S/358

Falas (Coast). The western shores of Beleriand. S/58

falassë *Q* 'coast', 'shore', 'line of surf'. S/358

falath *S* 'coast', 'shore', 'line of surf'. S/358

Falathar *S* (Lord of the Coast). A companion of Eärendil. **falath** = coast, **ar** = high, noble, royal. S/248

Falathrim *S* (Shore Host). The Telerin Elves of the Falas. **falath** = coast, **rim** = host. S/58

falma 'crested wave'. S/358

falma-li-nnar *Q* 'foaming waves many upon'. R/59

Falmari (Those of the Waves). The Sea Elves, a name for the Teleri. **falma** = crested wave. S/53

fan *S* 'cloud'. R/66

fân *S* 'cloud'. R/66

Fanuilos *S* 'bright angelic figure ever white as snow'. A title of the Vala Varda, usually translated as 'Snow White'. **fana** = figure, **ui** = ever, **los** = snow-white. R/66

fana *Q* 'veil', 'figure'. The radiant figure assumed by a Vala. Compare *S* **fan** = cloud. R/66

fan(g) *S* (beard). Compare *S* **fan** = cloud. See **Fangorn** = Treebeard.

Fangorn *S* 'Beard of Tree'. 3/409

Fanuidhol *S* 'Cloudyhead'. **fan** = cloud, **-ui** = adjective suffix, **dhol** = head. 1/296

fanyar *Q* 'clouds'. Singular **fana.** R/58

Faramir (Jeweled Hunter). The son of King Ondoher of Gondor. **far** from **faroth** = hunt, **mir** = jewel. 3/329

Faramir (Jeweled Hunter). The son of Denethor II, Steward of Gondor and Prince of Ithilien. 3/319

Faramir Took (Jeweled Hunter). The son of Peregrin Took. 3/381

faroth *S* 'hunt', 'pursue'. S/358

faug 'gape'. S/358

fëa 'spirit'. S/358

Fëanáro 'Spirit of Fire'. *Q* form of the name Fëanor. **fëa** = spirit, **nar** = fire. S/330

Fëanor 'Spirit of Fire'. The greatest of the Eldar, creator of the Silmarilli. **fëa** = spirit, **nor** = fire. 3/313

Fëanturi 'Masters of Spirits'. The Valar Mandos and Lórien. **fëa** = spirit, **tur** = master. S/28

Felagund 'Cave-hewer'. Called 'Lord of Caves' from *K* **felek-gundu** = cave-hewer. A title of Finrod. S/330

Fen Hollen 'The Closed Door'. The door to the cemetery behind Minas Tirith. **fen** from **fennas** = gateway, **hollen** = closed. 3/99

fennas *S* 'gateway'. R/66

fim (slim, slender). See following entry.

Fimbrethil 'Slim-Birch', 'Slender-Beech'. An Ent-wife called Wand-limb. 3/409

fin 'hair'. S/358

Fináráto (Champion [with Golden] Hair). A form of the name **Finrod**. **fin** = hair, **aráto** = champion. S/356

Finarfin (Hair Royal Hair). A son of Finwë. **fin** = hair, **ar** = high, noble, royal. S/60

Finarphir The royal house to which Galadriel and her brother Finrod Felegund belonged. **fin** = hair, **ar** = high, noble, royal. 3/406

Findegil (Star Hair). The scribe to King Eldarion. **fin** = hair, **gil** = star. 1/28

Finduilas (Leaf-flow Hair). The daughter of Orodreth. **fin** = hair, **dui** = flow, **las** = leaf. S/209

Finduilas (Leaf-flow Hair). The mother of Boromir and Faramir. 3/239

Finglas 'Leaflock'. An Ent. **fin** = hair, **las** = leaf. 2/77

Fingolfin (Cloak of Hair). A son of Finwë. **fin** = hair, **gollo** = cloak. S/60

Fingon (Commander [with Golden] Hair). The father of

Gil-galad. **fin** = hair, **gon** = commander. S/60

Finrod Felagund (Champion [with Golden] Hair) 'Lord of Caves'. Elven King of Nargothrond. See **Finaráto** = Champion with Golden Hair and **Felagund** = Cave Hewer. 1/89

Finwë (Hair). King of the Noldor in the Blessed Realm. **fin** = hair. S/52

fir (mortal). See following entries.

Firiel (Mortal Maiden). The daughter of King Ondoher of Gondor. **fir** = mortal, **-iel** = feminine name suffix. 3/329

Fírimar 'Mortals'. An Elvish name for Men. **-rim** = host, **-r** = plural suffix. S/103

firith *S* 'fading'. *Q* **quellë**. Autumn, the fourth season in the Elvish six-season year. 3/387

firn *S* (dead). See **Dor Firn-i-Guinar,** 'Land of the Dead that Live'.

Fladrif *S* 'Skinbark'. An Ent. 2/78

for *S* 'north'. S/360

Forgoil *D* 'Strawheads'. An epithet for the Rohirrim. 3/408

Forlindon The land north of the Gulf of Lune. **for** = north, **lin** = song, **don** = lofty. 1/00

Forlond (North Haven). A northern harbor on the Gulf of Lune. **for** = north, **lond** = haven. 1/00.

Forlong *PN* Lord of Lossarnach. 3/43

formen *Q* 'north'. The name of the Quenya letter *f.* 3/401

Formenos 'Northern Fortress' of Fëanor in the north of Valinor. **formen** = north, **os(t)** = fortress. S/71

forn *S* 'north'. S/358

Fornost Erain *S* 'Norbury of the Kings'. The seat of the Kings of Arthedain. **forn** = north, **ost** = fortress, **erain** = kings. 3/273

Forochel (Northern Ice). A northern cape and ice-bay. **forod** = north, **hel** = ice. 3/321

forod *S* 'north'. 3/401

Forodwaith (North People). Lands north of the Gray Mountains. **forod** = north, **waith** = people. 3/321

fuin *S* 'gloom'. S/360

Fuinur (Lover of Gloom). A Númenorean who joined the Haradrim. **fuin** = gloom, **nur** = lover of. S/293

Fundinûl *K* 'Son of Fundin'. **ul** = of. 1/333

G

g *S* Augmentive prefix to L as in **glos** and **glor.** R/62

Gabilgathol *K* Name for Belegost 'Great Fortress'. S/91

gaer *S* 'sea'. From **gaya** = awe, dread. S/359

Gaerys *S* A name for Ossë, the Maia of the Sea. S/359

gal *S* 'shine'. S/360

Galabas *H* 'Gamwich'. A form of the name Gamgee. 3/416

galad *S* 'radiance'. From **kal** = light. S/360

galadh *S* 'tree'. 3/388

galadhad *S* 'trees'. 3/388

galadhremmin ennorath 'treewoven lands of Middle-earth'. **galadh** = tree, **rem** = net, mesh, **en** = middle, **nor** = land, **ath** = collective plural suffix. R/64

Galadhriel (Tree Maiden). A form of the name Galadriel. **galadh** = tree, **riel** = garlanded maiden. S/360

Galadriel *S* 'Maiden Crowned with a Radiant Garland'. The Lady of the Galadrim, a name referring to her hair, which was compared to the Golden Tree. **galad** = radiance, **riel** = garlanded maiden, from **rig** = wreathe. 1/368, S/360

Galadrim *S* 'Tree-people'. The Elves of Lórien. **ga-**

ladh = tree, **galad** = light, **rim** = host. 1/355

Galathilion (White Shining Tree). The White Tree of Tirion. **galadh** = tree, **galad** = radiance, **thil** = shine with white or silver light, **-ion** = masculine name suffix. 3/250

Galbasi *H* 'Gammidgy'. An archaic form of the name Gamgee. 3/416

Galdor (Shining Lord). The father of Húrin and Huor. **gal** = shine, **dor** from **tar** = lord. S/148

Galdor (Shining Lord). An Elf of the Gray Havens. 1/253

galen *S* 'green'. S/360

galenas *S* (greens). Pipeweed. **galen** = green. 3/146

Galion (Bright). The butler of Thranduil in Mirkwood. **gal** = shine, **-ion** = masculine name suffix. H/193

Galpsi *H* 'Gamgee'. 3/416

galvorn (shining black). The black, shining, supple metal invented by and worn by Eöl the Dark Elf. **gal** = shine, **vorn** = black. S/133

ganta T/76

gaur 'werewolf'. S/359

gaya 'awe', 'dread'. S/359

gebir 'stakes'. S/364

gelin *S* 'green'. Singular **galen.** S/360

Gelion (Flowing). The main river of the seven rivers of Ossiriand. **kel** = flow, **-ion** = place name suffix. S/54

Gelmir (Flowing Jewel). An Elf of Nargothrond. **gel** from **kel** = flow, **mir** = jewel. S/188

Gelmir (Flowing Jewel). An Elf of Angrod's folk. S/212

gelyd *S* 'wise'. Plural form of the word **Noldo.** S/359

gerthas *S* 'runes'. S/360

Ghân-buri-Ghân *W* The headman of the Woses. 3/105

ghâsh *B* 'fire'. 1/341

gil *S* 'star', 'bright spark'. R/65

giliath *S* 'star host'. **-ath** = collective plural suffix. S/359

Gil-Estel 'Star of Hope'. *S* name for Eärendil as a star. **gil** = star, **estel** = hope. S/250

Gil-galad 'Star of Bright Light', 'Star of Radiance'. A high king of the Noldor. **gil** = star, **galad** = radiance. S/154

Gildor *S* (Starlord). A companion of Barahir. **gil** = star, **dor** from **tar** = lord. S/155

Gildor Inglorion *S* (Starlord). An Elf of the house of Finrod. **gil** = star, **dor** = lord, **glor** = golden. 1/89

Gilraen (Wandering Star). The mother of Aragorn. **gil** = star, **ran** = wander. 3/338

Gilrain (Wandering Star). A river in Gondor. The name is listed as **Gilraen** on S/163. 3/151

Gilthoniel *S* 'Star-kindler'. A title of the Vala Varda. R/64

gimbatul *B* 'to find them'. 1/267

Gimilkhâd *N* The father of Ar-Pharazôn. S/269

Ginglith A river tributary to the Narog. **lith** = ash. S/169

gir 'ship'. From **cir**. See **Pelargir** 'The Garth of Royal Ships'. S/360

Girion (Lord of Ships). A Lord of Dale, ancestor of Bard the Bowman. **gir** = ship, **-ion** masculine name suffix. H/271

girith 'shuddering'. S/359

Girithron *S* (Great Shuddering). *Q* **Ringarë,** the month corresponding to December. 3/388

glam 'din'. S/360

glamhoth 'din-horde'. A name for Orcs. S/360

Glamdring 'Foe-Hammer'. Gandalf's Elven Sword. Refers to the **glamhoth** = Orcs. 1/293

Glanduin (Falling River). A river tributary to the Greyflood. **lanta** = fall, **duin** = large river. 3/319

Glaurung A dragon, called 'the Worm of Morgoth'. **laur** = golden. S/116

glîn 'gleam', particularly the gleam of eyes. S/359

Glingal 'Hanging Flame'. The image of the Golden Tree in Gondolin. **glin** = gleam, **gal** = shine. S/126

Glirhuin (Song of Darkness). A minstrel. **lir** from **lin** = song, **huin** = darkness. S/230

glob *B,* as in **Saruman-glob.** 2/48

glor *S* 'gold in color or light'. S/361

Glóredhel (Golden Elf). Daughter of Hador. **glor** = golden, **edhel** = elf. S/158

Glorfindel 'Golden Haired'. An Elf of Gondolin. **glor** = golden, **fin** = hair, **el** = elf. S/194

Glorfindel 'Golden Haired'. An Elven Lord of Elrond's household. 1/222

glos 'dazzling white'. R/62

Golasgil The Lord of Anfalas. **las** = leaf, **gil** = star. 3/43

Golfimbul *O* An Orc King. A pun on golf in *The Hobbit.* Norse *fimbul* = an element in names of supernatural things. H/26

golodh *S* 'knowledge', 'wisdom'. S/356

Golodhrim *S* Noldor. **golodh** = wisdom, **rim** = host. S/134

gollo 'cloak'. S/365

gon 'commander'. From **káno.** S/360

gon *S* 'stone'. S/359

gond *S* 'stone'. S/359

Gondolin 'The Hidden Rock'. King Turgon's hidden city. **gond** = stone, **dolen** = hidden. 1/256

Gondolindrim The people of Gondolin. S/138

Gondor 'Land of Stone'. The South Kingdom. **gon** = stone, **dor** = land. 1/256

Gonnhirrim 'Masters of Stone'. *S* name for Dwarves.

gon = stone, **hir** = lord, **rim** = host. S/91

gor 'horror', 'dread'. S/359

Gorbag *O, B* An Orc. 2/344

Gorbag *O, B* An Orc-captain. 3/175

Gorgoroth (Place of Horror). The plateau of Mordor. **gorgor** = horror. 1/258

górgûn *W* 'Orcs'. 3/106

Gorlim A companion of Barahir. **gor** = horror, dread. S/155

goroth 'horror', 'dread'. S/359

Gorthaur (Dread Abomination). S name of Sauron. **gor** = horror, **thaur** = abominable. S/32

Gorthol 'Dread Helm'. A name of Turin. **gor** = dread, **thol** = helm. S/205

Gothmog The Lord of the Balrogs. **goth** = enemy. S/107

Gothmog The Lieutenant of Minas Morgul. 3/121

govannen In *Mae govannen!* 1/222

Gram A mountain, dwelling place of Orcs. H/26

Grishnákh *O* An Orc. 2/49

grist 'cleave'. From **kir** = cut, cleave. S/363

grod 'delving', 'underground dwelling'. S/359

Grond The Mace of Morgoth, the Hammer of the Underworld. S/154

Grond The battering ram used against Minas Tirith. 3/102

groth *S* 'delving', 'underground dwelling'. S/359

Guilin (Song of Awakening). An Elf of Nargothrond. **cuivë** = awakening, **lin** = song. S/188

guinar 'live'. See **Dor Firn-i-Guinar,** 'Land of the Dead that Live'. S/357

gûl 'sorcery'. From **ngol** = lore, darkened through association with **morgul** = black arts. S/359

Gundor A son of Hador. S/148

Gundabad One of the northernmost Misty Mountains, a dwelling place for Orcs. 1/oo.

gurth *S* 'death'. S/359

Gurthang *S* 'Iron of Death'. Beleg's sword Anglachel reforged for Túrin. **gurth** = death, **anga** = iron. S/201

gwae *S* (wind). See following entries.

Gwaeron *S* (Great Wind). *Q* **Sulime,** the month corresponding to March. 3/388

gwai *S* (wind). See following entry.

Gwaihir *S* 'Windlord'. The Lord of the Eagles. **gwai** = wind, **hir** = lord. 1/275

gwaith *S* 'people'. S/359

Gwaith-i-Mírdain *S* 'People of the Jewelsmiths'. The craftsmen of Eregion, of whom Celebrimbor was most skilled. **gwaith** = people, **mir** = jewel, **dain** = wrights, smiths. S/286

gwath *S* 'shadow', 'dimness'. S/359

Gwathlo The Greyflood River. **gwath** = shadow. 1/oo.

Gwindor An Elf of Nargothrond. S/188

Gwirith *S* The month that corresponds with April. *Q* **Viressë.** 3/388

H

hadhod *S* Form of **khazad** 'Dwarves'. S/359

Hadhodrond *S* Name for Khazad-dûm, Moria. **rond** = delvings. S/91

Hador Founder of the Third House of the Edain. 1/284

Haerast 'The Far Shore'. The coast of Aman the Blessed. **rast** = coast. S/343

hain *S* (them). 1/319

Haladin The second group of Men to enter Beleriand. S/142

Halbarad Dúnadan (Tall-tower Man of the West). A Ranger of the north, Aragorn's standard-bearer. **halla** = tall, **barad** = tower, **Dúnadan** = Man of the West. 3/47

Haldad A leader of the Haladin. S/145

Haldan (Tall Smith). A leader of the Haladin. **halla** = tall, **dan** = wright, smith. S/146

Haldar Son of Haldad of the Haladin. S/146

Haldir (Tall Watcher). Son of Halmir of the Haladin. **halla** = tall, **dir** = watch. S/158

Haldir (Tall Watcher). An Elven guard on the borders of Lórien. 1/357

Haleth Lady Haleth, leader of the Haladin, who were so named in her honor. S/195

halla *Q* 'tall'. The name of the Quenya letter used to represent a voiceless consonant. 3/401

Hallas (Tall Leaf). The thirteenth Ruling Steward of Gondor. **halla** = tall, **las** = leaf. 3/319

Halmir *S* (Tall Jewel). A leader of the Haladin. **halla** = tall, **mir** = jewel. S/195

Handir A leader of the Haladin. **dir** = watch. S/195

har *S* 'south'. S/360

harad *S* 'south'. 3/401

Haradrim *S* 'Southrons, People of the South'. **harad** = south, **rim** = host. 1/258

Haradwaith *S* (South People). The lands south of Gondor and Mordor. **harad** = south, **waith** = people. 1/00

haranyë The last year of a century. Compare **yen** = long year. 3/386

Hareth The mother of Húrin and Huor. S/158

Harlindon (South Lindon). The lands south of the gulf of Lune. **har** = south, **lin** = song, wave, **don** = lofty. 1/00

Harlond *S* (South Haven). A harbor in the south of the

Gulf of Lune. **har** = south, **lond** = haven. 3/331

Harlond *S* (South Haven). A landing on the Anduin south of Minas Tirith. 3/22

harma *Q* 'treasure'. The name of the Quenya letter *hk*. 3/401

harn *S* 'south'. S/360

Harnen *S* (Southwater). A river south of Gondor. **har** = south, **nen** = water. 3/325

Harondor *S* 'South Gondor'. **har** = south. 1/00

Hathaldir A companion of Barahir. S/155

Hathol The father of Hador. **thol** = helm. S/147

haudh *S* 'mound'. S/359

Haudh-en-Arwen 'The Ladybarrow'. The burial mound of Haleth in the forest of Brethil. **haudh** = mound, **en** = of the, **Arwen** = royal maiden. S/147

Haudh-en-Elleth (Mound of the Elf-maid). The burial mound of Finduilas. S/216

Haudh-in-Gwanûr Burial mound of the twin brothers Folcred and Fastred of Rohan. 3/335

Haudh-en-Ndengin 'Mound of the Slain'. The burial mound of Elves and Men dead in the Nirnaeth Arnoediad. S/197

Haudh-en-Nirnaeth 'The Mound of Tears'. A name for the **Haudh-en-Ndengin.** S/197

Helcar (The Ice). The inland sea in ancient Middle-earth. **helka** = ice. S/49

Helcaraxë (Ice Jaws). The icy strait in the north between the Blessed Realm and Middle-earth. **helka** = ice, **caraxë** from **carag** = jaws. S/51

heledh *S* 'glass'. From *K* **kheled**. S/360

Helevorn 'Black Glass'. A lake in Thargelion. **heledh** = glass, **vorn** = black. S/112

helka *Q* 'icy', 'ice-cold'. S/360

Helluin (Blue Ice). The star Sirius, which shines blue. **helka** = ice, **luin** = blue. S/48

hen *S* (eye). See **Amon Hen,** 'Hill of the Eye', and **Henneth Annûn.**

Henneth Annûn *S* 'Window of the Sunset'. Cave and waterfall in Ithilien. **annûn** = west, sunset. 2/282

Herion *S* (Son of Lords). The third Ruling Steward of Gondor. **heru** = lord, **-ion** = masculine name suffix, son of. 3/319

heru *Q* 'lord'. S/359

Herumor *Q* (Dark Lord). A Númenorean who joined the Haradrim. **heru** = lord, **mor** = dark. S/293

Herunúmen *Q* 'Lord of the West'. *Q* name of Ar-Adûnakhor. **heru** = lord, **númen** = west. S/269

hi *S* In *Edro hi ammen!* 1/320

hil (follow, heir). S/317

hildinyar *Q* 'heirs'. 3/245

Hildor 'The Followers', 'The Aftercomers'. An Elvish name for Men. S/99

Hildorien (Land of the Followers). The land where Men **Hildor** first awoke. **-ien** = a place name suffix. S/103

him 'cool'. S/359

Himlad 'Cool Plain' where Celegorm and Curufin lived. **him** = cool, **lad** = plain. S/143

Himring 'Evercold'. A hill where Maedhros had his stronghold. **him** = cool, **ring** = cold. S/112

hin (these). 1/319

híni 'children'. S/359

hir 'river'. S/364

hîr *S* 'lord'. S/359

hiril *S* 'lady'. S/359

Hírilorn *S* 'Tree of the Lady'. The tree in which Lúthien was imprisoned. **hiril** = lady, **orn** = tree. S/172

hir-uva *Q* 'find-will'. R/59

hir-uva-lye *Q* 'find wilt thou'. R/59

Hirgon (Lord Commander). An errand rider from Gondor to Rohan. **hir** = lord, **gon** = commander. 3/72

Hirluin (Lord of the Blue). The Lord of the Green Hills of Pinnath Gelin. **hir** = lord, **luin** = blue. 3/43

hísië *Q* 'mist'. R/59

Hísilómë *Q* 'Land of Mist'. Name for Hithlum. **hísië** = mist, **lómë** = shadow. S/118

hith *S* 'mist'. S/359

Hithaiglir 'Line of Misty Peaks'. The Misty Mountains. The spelling **Hithaiglin** (1/00) is in error. **hith** = mist, **ai** = peaks. S/54

hithlain *S* 'mist-thread'. A type of rope made by the Elves of Lórien. 1/388

Hithlum *S* 'Land of Mist'. A name for Hísilómë. **hith** = mist, **lum** = shadow. S/51

Hithui *S* (misty). *Q* **Hisie.** The month corresponding to November. **hith** = mist, **-ui** = adjective suffix. 3/388

hloth *H* 'cottage'. A two-roomed dwelling. 3/416

Hlothram *H* 'Cotman'. An early form of the surname Cotton. 3/416

Hlothrama *H* 'Cottager'. An early form of the surname Cotton. 3/416

Hlothran *H* 'Cot-town', 'Cot-ton'. 3/416

hollen *S* (closed). See **Fen Hollen** = the Closed Door.

hoth *S* 'host', 'horde'. Usually in a bad sense. S/360

hrivë *Q* 'winter'. *S* **rhîw.** The fifth season of the Elvish six-season year. 3/386

Huan 'Great dog', 'Hound'. The hound that aided Lúthien. S/172

huinë *Q* 'gloom', 'darkness'. S/358

Hunthor A man of the Haladin. **thor** = torrent. S/221

Huor The father of Tuor. 3/314

huorn Ents that have become nearly like trees. **orn** = tree. 2/170

Húrin A hero, the father of Túrin. S/126

Húrin The Warden of the Keys in Minas Tirith. 3/121

hwesta *Q* 'breeze'. The name of the Quenya letter *hw*. 3/401

hyarmen *Q* 'south'. The name of the Quenya letter *h* or *hy*. 3/401

Hyarmendacil *Q* 'South-victor'. The name taken by Kings of Gondor who defeated the Southrons. **hyarmen** = south, **dacil** = victor. 3/325

Hyarmentir *Q* (Watcher of the South). The highest mountain in the south of Valinor. **hyarmen** = south, **tir** = watch. S/74

I

i *Q* (the). R/59

i *S* (that). S/188

iâ 'void', 'abyss'. S/360

iant *S* 'bridge'. *Q* **yanta.** S/360

Iant Iaur 'The Old Bridge' over the Esgalduin River. **iant** = bridge, **iaur** = old. S/121

iar 'old'. S/360

Iarwain Ben-adar Bombadil, oldest and fatherless, Master of the lands around the Old Forest. **iar** = old, **adar** = father. 1/278

iach (ford). See **Brithiach** and **Arossiach.**

iâth 'fence'. S/360

iaur 'old'. S/360

iavas *S* 'autumn'. *Q* **yávië.** The third season of the Elvish six-season year. 3/386

Ibun A son of Mîm, the Petty Dwarf. S/203

Idril Celebrindal (Sparkling Brilliance Silver-foot). Tuor's Elven wife, daughter of Turgon, mother of Eärendil. *Q* **Itarillë** or **Itarilde** from **ita** = to sparkle, **ril** = brilliance, **celebrin** = silver-like, **dal** = foot. 3/314

-iel feminine name suffix, translated 'daughter of' and 'maiden'.

-iel verb suffix.

-ien feminine name suffix.

Illuin (Blue Star). The northern Lamp of the Valar. **el** = star, **luin** = blue. S/35

Ilmarë (Star Home). A Maia, handmaid to Varda. **el** = star, **mar** = home. S/30

Ilmarin 'Mansion of the High Airs'. The strand of Valinor. **el** = star, **mar** = home, dwelling. 1/247

Ilmen 'the region of stars'. The upper sky. S/99

ilúvë *Q* 'the all', 'the whole'. S/360

Ilúvatar *Q* 'The Father of All'. Eru, the One. **ilúvë** = all, **atar** = father. S/15

ilye *Q* 'all', plural. R/59

im *S* 'I'. 1/319

im *S* (between). See **Taur-im-Duinath** 'Forest between Rivers' and **imbe.**

imbe *Q* 'between'. R/59

Imlach (Leaping Flame of Stars). The father of Amlach. The name may be in an untranslatable human language. S/144

imlad 'deep valley'. Compare **imbe** = between, **lad** = plain. 3/433

Imlad Morgûl (Valley of Sorcery). The valley where Minas Morgul stood. **morgûl** = black arts. 2/303

Imladris 'Deep Dale of the Cleft'. Rivendell. **ris** = cleave. 1/259

Imloth Melui (Between the Golden Flowers). A land in

fief to Gondor. **imbe** = between, **loth** = blossoms, **mel** = gold, **-ui** = adjective suffix. 3/142

Imrahil *N* The Prince of Dol Amroth. 3/22

in (of the). See various place names, including **Haudh-in-Gwanur.**

Indis The mother of Fingolfin and Finarfin. S/60

Ingold A man of Minas Tirith. 3/21

Ingwë The leader of the Vanyar, considered High King over all the Elves. S/52

inzil *N* (flower). See **Rothinzil** 'Foamflower'.

Inziladun *N* (Flower of the West). Name of Tar-Palantir, S/269

Inzilbêth *N* The queen of Ar-Gimilzôr. S/268

-ion Masculine name suffix, sometimes translated as 'son of'.

-ion Place name suffix.

Ioreth (Old One). The eldest healing-woman of Minas Tirith. **iar** = old. 3/136

Irmo 'Desirer' or 'Master of Desire'. The Vala usually called Lórien. S/28

Iorlas (Old Leaf). Bergil's uncle. **iar** = old, **las** = leaf. 3/42

Isil *Q* 'moon', 'The Sheen'. *S* **Ithil.** 3/392, S/99

Isildur *Q* (Lover of the Moon). A son of Elendil. **isil** = moon, **dur** = friend, lover. 3/318

Isilya *Q* 'Moonday'. 3/388

Istari 'wizards'. 3/365

Ithil *S* 'Moon'. *Q* **Isil.** 3/392

ithildin *S* 'starmoon'. **ithil** = moon, **din** from **tinwe** = star, spark. 1/218

-ith '-ing'. S/364

Ithilien (Moonland). The eastern region of Gondor. 1/258

Ivanneth *S* 'giver of fruits'. *Q* **Yavannië.** The month corresponding to September. 3/388

Ivorwen *S* The maternal grandmother of Aragorn. **wen** = maiden. 3/388

Ivren The lake and falls at the source of the river Narog. S/119

K

kal *S* 'shine'. S/360

kambâ 'hand'. S/356

káno 'commander'. S/360

Karnevalinar (Red Power-flame). **cärne** = red, **val** = power, **nar** = fire. T/76

Karningul *C* Rivendell. 3/412

kast *H* 'mathom'. A thing the use of which is forgotten. 3/414

kastu *R* 'mathom'. 3/415

kel 'go away', 'flow away', 'flow down'. S/360

Kelos (Flowing Snow). A river in Gondor. **kel** = flow, **los** = snow. 3/00.

kelvar 'animals', 'living things that move'. From **kel**. S/45

kemen *Q* 'the earth'. S/360

Kementári *Q* 'Queen of the Earth'. A title of the Vala Yavanna. **kemen** = earth, **tári** = queen. S/28

Khand The eastern land from which the Variags came. 3/121

Khazâd *K* 'Dwarves'. 3/411

Khazâd-aimênu! *K* 'The Dwarves are upon you!' 3/411

Khazâd-dûm *K* 'Dwerrowdelf', 'The Mansions of the Dwarves'. Moria. 1/253

kheled *K* 'glass'. S/360

Kheled-zâram *K* 'Mirrormere'. Literally, 'Glass Lake', the lake east of Moria. 1/296

khelek *S* 'ice'. S/360

khil 'follow'. S/360

Khîm *K* A son of Mîm, the Petty-Dwarf. S/203

Khuzdul *K* The Dwarvish language. **Khazâd** = Dwarves, **-ul** = of. 3/392

Kibil-nâla *K* 'Silverlode'. *S* Celebrant. 1/296

kir 'cut', 'cleave'. S/360

Kiril (Cleft of the Stars). A river in Gondor. **kir** = cleave, **el** = star, **ril** = brilliance. 3/00

Kôr (One Who Rises). A mountain. Compare **Melkor** = He who arises in might. T/77

krimpatul *B* 'to bind them'. 1/267

kris 'cut', 'cleave'. From **kir** = cut, cleave. S/363

Kud-dukan *R* 'Hole-dweller'. Hobbit. 3/416

Kuduk *H* 'Hobbit'. 3/416

kuluvi *Q* Compare **cul** = golden-red. T/76

L

lach 'leaping flame'. S/361

lad 'plain', 'valley'. S/361

Ladros (Plain of Foam). The lands given to the Men of the House of Beor. **lad** = plain, **ros** = foam. S/148

laer *S* 'summer'. Perhaps literally 'green'. See **Corollaire**, 'The Green Mound'. *Q* **lairë,** the second season in the Elvish six-season year. 3/386

Laer Cú Beleg 'The Song of the Great Bow' sung in memory of the archer Beleg, known as Cúthalion 'Strongbow'. Because **Beleg** = great, mighty, the title can also mean the Song of the Bow of Beleg. S/209

Lagduf *O, B.* An Orc. 3/182

lain *S* (thread). See **hithlain** = mist-thread.

Laiquendi 'The Green Elves' of Ossiriand. **lai,** see **lairë, quendi** = Elves, literally, 'speakers'. S/96

lairë *Q* 'summer'. Perhaps literally 'green'. See **Corollairë** 'The Green Mound.' *S* **laer,** the second season of the Elvish six-season year. 3/386

laite *Q* (praise). 3/231

laituvalmet *Q* (praise will we). **laite** = praise, **-uva** = will, **met** = we two. 3/231

Lalaith 'Laughter'. A daughter of Húrin and Morwen. S/198

lambe *Q* 'tongue'. The name of the Quenya letter *l.* 3/401

Lamedon A land in fief to Gondor. 3/43

lammen *S* 'voice'. 1/320

Lammoth 'The Great Echo'. A region in which remained the echoes of Morgoth's cries in his battle with Ungoliant. **lom** = echo. S/80

Landroval (Swooping Steed of Power). An eagle. **lanta** = fall, **roh** = horse, **val** = power. 3/226

lanta *Q* 'fall'. Noun. R/63

lantar *Q* 'fall'. Plural verb. R/58

Lanthir Lammath 'Waterfall of Echoing Voices'. Where Dior lived in Ossiriand. **lanta** = fall, **thir** from **sir** = stream, **lom** = echo, **-ath** = collective plural suffix. S/235

las (leaf). See following entries.

lasse-lanta *Q* 'leaf-fall', 'autumn'. **lasse** = leaf, **lanta** = fall. R/62

Lassemista (Gray-leaf). A rowan tree. **lasse** = leaf, **mista** from **mith** = gray. 2/87

lassi *Q* 'leaves'. R/58

lasto *S* 'listen'. S/363

laurë *Q* 'golden'. Golden in light or color rather than referring to metallic gold. R/62

laurea *Q* 'golden'. R/62

Laurelin *Q* 'Song of Gold'. The Golden Tree. **laurë** = golden, **lin** = song. 3/314

Laurelindorinan *Q* 'Land of the Valley of the Singing Gold'. The original name of Lórien. **laurë** = gold, **lin** = song, **dor** = land, **nan** = valley. 2/70

laurie *Q* 'golden'. R/62

le *S* 'thee'. R/64

Lebennin A large land in fief to Gondor. **nin** = water. 1/309

lebethron A beautiful type of black wood. 3/245

Lefnui A river in southwest Gondor. **-ui** = adjective suffix. 1/00.

Legolas An Elf, son of Thranduil, one of the Fellowship of the Ring. **las** = leaf. 2/106

Legolin One of the seven rivers of Ossiriand. **lin** = song. S/123

Leithian 'Release from Bondage'. The Lay of Leithian recounts the tale of Beren and Lúthien. S/162

lembas, len-bas 'waybread'. An unusually sustaining bread for travelers, given by Melian and by Galadriel. 3/438

Lenwë The leader of the Nandor, the Elves who turned back at the Misty Mountains. S/54

leuca *Q* 'snake'. *S* **lyg.** 3/393

lhach 'leaping flame'. S/361

lhaw *S* (hearing, ear). See **Amon Lhaw,** the Hill of Hearing.

lhûg *S* 'snake', 'serpent'. S/361

Lhun (Blue). A gulf, river, and mountains in the west of Eriador. **luin** = blue. 1/00.

lin *S* 'pool', 'mere'. S/361

lin 'sing', 'make a musical sound'. S/361

Linaewen 'Lake of Birds'. A great lake in Nevrast. **lin** = pool, **aewë** = bird. S/119

lindë *Q* 'singing', 'song'. S/361

lindelorendor *Q* (singing golden land). Treebeard's description of Lórien. **linde** = singing, **lor** from **laurë** = gold, **dor** = land. 2/70

Lindir (Singing Watcher). An Elf of Elrond's household. **lin** = sing, **dir** = watch. 1/249

Lindon (Lofty Song) (Lofty Wave). The land between Ered Luin and the sea after the First Age. **lin** = song, wave, **don** = lofty. 3/320

Lindórië (Lady of Song). The mother of Inzilbêth in Númenor. **lin** = song, **dor** = lord. S/268

Linhir (Song Lord, Song of the River). A town on the river Gilraen in Gondor. **lin** = song, **hîr** = lord, **hir** = river. 3/151

linnar *Q* 'waves-many-upon'. R/58

linnathon *S* 'I will chant'. From **lin** = song. R/64

linnod A couplet, perhaps with internal rhyme only. Compare **lin** = song. 3/342

linte *Q* 'swift'. R/58

lintulinda (swiftly sing). **linte** = swift, **lin** = song. T/76

lirinen *Q* 'song-in'. R/58

Lissi *Q* 'sweet'. R/58

lith 'ash'. S/361

Lithlad 'Plain of Ashes' in Mordor. **lith** = ash, **lad** = plain. 2/244

loa 'growth'. A solar year, the time for a cycle of growth in plants. 3/385

Loeg Ningloron *S* 'Pools of the Golden Water-Flowers'. The Gladden Fields where flag-lilies *(ME gladdon)* grew. **nin** = water, **glor** = golden. S/338

loende (Midyearsday). **loa** = growth, a year, **end** = middle. 3/386

lok 'bend', 'loop'. From *Q* **hlokë** = snake, serpent. S/361

lóm 'echo'. S/361

lómë 'dusk'. S/361

Lómeänor *Q* 'Gloomyland'. Entwood. **lómeä** = gloomy from **lómë** = dusk, **nor** = land. 3/409

lomelindi *Q* 'dusk singers'. A poetic name for nightingales. **lómë** = dusk, **lindi** = singers from **lin** = song. S/55

Lómion *Q* 'Son of Twilight'. A name of Maeglin. **lómë** = twilight, **-ion** = masculine name suffix, son of. S/133

lond *S* 'landlocked haven'. S/361

Lond Daer (Shadowed Haven) at the mouth of the Gwathlo. **lond** = haven, **dae** = shadow. o/oo

londë *Q* 'landlocked haven'. S/361

lonn 'landlocked haven'. S/361

lor *S* 'golden' in color or light. S/361

Lórellin (Lake of the Stars of Gold). A lake in Lórien in Valinor. **lór** = gold, **el** = star, **lin** = lake. S/28

Lorgan A chief of the Easterlings. S/238

Lórien (Golden). A name of the Vala Irmo and of his dwelling place. S/25

Lórien (Golden). The Golden Wood of Galadriel. 1/239

Lóriendesse *Q* 'in Lórien'. R/58

Lorindol 'Goldenhead'. A name of Hador. **lor** = golden, **dol** = head. S/338

los 'snow'. S/361

Losgar (Red Snow). The place where Feanor burned the ships of the Teleri. **los** = snow, **gar** from **car** = red. S/90

loss *S* 'snow'. R/61

Loss-hoth *S* 'Snowmen'. People who lived on the Ice-

Bay of Forochel. **loss** = snow, **hoth** = host. R/62

Lossarnach A land in the southern White Mountains. **loss** = snow. 3/22

losse *Q* 'fallen snow', 'snow-white'. R/61

lossen *S* 'snowy'. R/61

Lossoth *S* 'Snowmen'. People who lived on the Ice-Bay of Forochel. **loss** = snow, **hoth** = host. R/62

lost (empty). See **Camlost** 'Empty-handed'.

lótë *Q* 'flower', 'blossom'. S/361

Lótessë *Q* (In Blossom). *S* **Lothron**. The month that corresponds to May. **lótë** = blossom, **-esse** = in. 3/388

loth *S* 'flower', 'blossom'. S/361

Lothiriel *S* (Flower-garlanded Maiden). The daughter of Prince Imrahil of Dol Amroth, wedded to Eomer of Rohan. **loth** = flower, **riel** = garlanded maiden. 3/352

Lothlann A great plain called 'the Wide and Empty'. S/123

Lothlórien (Golden Flower). The Golden Wood of Galadriel. **loth** = flower, **lórien** = dream. 1/349

Lothron (Flowery). *Q* **Lótessë**. The month corresponding to May. **loth** = flower. 3/388

lug *B* (tower). See following entry.

Lugburz *B* 'Dark Tower'. Sauron's tower Barad-dûr in Mordor. **lug** = tower, **burz** = dark. 2/49

Lugdush *B* An Orc of the White Hand. **lug** = tower. 2/64

luin 'blue'. S/361

luine *Q* 'river'. Compare *S* **duinē** 'river'. C/179

luini *Q* 'blue'. R/58

Luinil (Blue Star). A blue-shining star. **luin** = blue, **il** from **el** = star. S/48

Lumbar (Shadowhome). A star. **lómë** = dusk, **bar** from **mar** = home. S/48

lumbule *Q* 'heavy shadow'. **lómë** = dusk. R/59

lúmenn' (hour). 1/90

Lúthien Tinuviel (Blossom Nightingale). The daughter of Thingol and Melian, wedded to Beren. **loth** = blossom, **-ien** = feminine name suffix, **tinuviel** = nightingale, literally 'Daughter of Twilight'. 1/206.

lúva *Q* 'bow'. The bow-shaped parts of the Tengwar letters. 3/398

lye *Q* (thou). R/59

lyg *S* 'snake'. *Q* **leuca.** 3/393

M

ma (hand). See following entries.

ma-r-ya-t *Q* 'hands-her-two'. **ma** = hand, **r** = plural suffix, **-t** = dual suffix. R/58

Mablung 'of the Heavy Hand'. An Elf of Doriath. **ma** = hand. S/113

Mablung 'of the Heavy Hand'. One of the Rangers of Ithilien. 2/267

mae In *Mae govannen!* 1/222

Maedhros A son of Fëanor. **ros** = foam. S/60

maeg *S* 'sharp', 'piercing'. S/361

Maeglin *S* 'Sharp Glance'. The son of Eöl and Aredhel. **maeg** = sharp, **glin** = gleam, as of eyes. S/92

Maglor (Goldenhand). A son of Fëanor. **ma** = hand, **glor** = golden. S/60

Magor (Hand of Dread). A son of Malach, a leader of Men. **ma** = hand, **gor** = dread. The name may be in an untranslatable human language. S/115

Mahal *K* The Dwarves' name for the Vala Aulë, who made them. S/44

Máhanaxar The Ring of Doom, the circle where the

thrones of the Valar were set for council. S/38

Mahtan A great smith of the Noldor. S/64

Maia Plural **Maiar.** Ainur (Holy Ones) of lesser power than the Valar. Gandalf (Olorin) and Sauron were Maiar. S/21

maika *Q* 'sharp', 'piercing'. S/361

maite (hand). See **morimaitesincahonda** = blackhanded (a description of Orcs) and **ma** = hand.

mal 'gold'. S/361

Malach (Hand of Leaping Flame). A son of Marach. **ma** = hand, **lach** = leaping flame. The name may be in an untranslatable human language. S/143

Malbeth (Gold Word). The Seer who foretold the return of the Dead and the end of Arvedui's line of kings. **mal** = gold, **beth** = word. 3/54

Malduin 'Yellow River'. A river tributary to the Teiglin. **mal** = gold, **duin** = large river. S/205

Malinalda 'Tree of Gold'. A name of the Golden Tree. **mal** = gold, **alda** = tree. S/38

Malinornelion (gold beech tree). Lothlórien. **mal** = gold, **orn** = tree, **neldor** = beech. 2/70

Mallor (Yellow Gold). The third King of Arthedain. **mal** = gold, **lór** = gold. 3/318

mallorn (gold tree). The golden trees of Lórien. **mal** = gold, **orn** = tree. 1/356

mallos (gold snow). The golden flowers of Lebennin. **mal** = gold, **los** = snow. 3/151

malta *Q* 'gold'. The name of the Quenya letter *m*. 3/401

Malvegil The fourth King of Arthedain. **mal** = gold, **gil** = star. 3/318

man *Q* 'who'. R/58

mān 'good', 'blessed', 'unmarred'. S/361

Mandos (Imprisonment). A name of the Vala Námo and of his dwelling place where the dead wait. **mbando** = prison, **os** = fortress. S/28

Manwë (Blessed). The Elder King of the Valar, Lord of the Air. S/21

már *Q* 'home', 'dwelling'. S/356

Marach Leader of the third migration of Men to enter Beleriand. S/142

Mar-nu-Falmar 'Land under the Waves'. A name of Númenor after its sinking. **mar** = dwelling, **nu** = under, **falmar** = waves. S/281

Mardil Voronwe 'Devoted to the House (of the Kings)'. The first Ruling Steward of Gondor. **mar** = home, **dil** = devoted to. 3/319

maruvan *Q* 'I will abide'. **mar** = dwell, **uva** = will. 3/245

Mauhur *O, B.* An Orc. 2/58

Mazarbul *K* 'Records'. 1/336

mbár 'home' of persons or peoples, an ancient word from which derived *Q* **már** and *S* **bar** 'home', 'dwelling'. S/356

mbando 'prison', 'duress'. The ancient word from which derived *Q* **mando** and *S* **band** 'prison', 'duress'. S/356

med (wet). See **Dolmed** = Wet Head.

megil (sword). See **Mormegil** 'Black Sword'.

mel (gold). Plural. See **mellyrn** = gold trees and **Imloth Melui** = Between the Golden Flowers.

mel 'love'. S/361

Melian *S* 'Dear Gift'. A Maia, mother of Lúthien, wedded to Thingol. From *Q* **Melyanna. mel** = love, **anna** = gift. 3/314

Melkor *Q* 'He Who Arises in Might'. The original Quenya name of Morgoth, the Great Enemy. **Mel** may be a form of **bel** = power. S/16

mellon *S* 'friend'. From **mel** = love. 1/321

mellyrn *S* (gold trees). The golden trees of Lórien. **mel** = gold (plural), **yrn** = trees (singular **orn**). 1/356

Melyanna *Q* 'Dear Gift'. The Quenya form of the name **Melian**. **mel** = love, **anna** = gift. S/361

men *Q* 'region', 'direction', 'way'. R/64

Menegroth 'The Thousand Caves'. The dwelling of Melian and Thingol. **groth** = underground dwelling. S/93

menel 'heaven'. From **men** = region, **el** = star. R/64

Meneldil (Lover of Heaven). The second King of Gondor, the son of Anarion. **menel** = heaven, **dil** = friend, lover of. 3/318

Meneldor (Heaven Lord). An Eagle of the Misty Mountains. **menel** = heaven, **dor** from **tar** = lord. 3/228

Menelmacar *Q* (Swordsman of the Sky). The constellation corresponding to Orion. *S* **Menelvagor**. **menel** = heaven. 3/391

Meneltarma *Q* 'Pillar of Heaven'. A mountain in Númenor from which Eresseä could be seen. **menel** = heaven, **tarma** = pillar. 3/315

Menelvagor *S* (Swordsman of the Sky). See *Q* **Menelmacar**. 3/391

Menelya *Q* 'Heavensday'. **menel** = heaven. 3/388

mereth 'feast'. S/361

Mereth Aderthad 'The Feast of Reuniting' held by Fingolfin. S/113

Merethrond 'Feast Hall' in the citadel of Minas Tirith. **mereth** = feast, **thrond** = hall. 3/253

met *Q* 'us two'. R/58

met (end). See following entries.

Methedras (Last Horn). Southernmost of the Misty Mountains. **met** = end, **ras** = horn. 2/32

mettarë *Q* (last light). The last day of the year. **met** = end, **árë** = sunlight. 3/386

mí *Q* 'in the'. R/58

Mîm The last Petty-dwarf. S/202

min An element appearing in the names of isolated and prominent things. Compare **minas** = tower. S/361

Min-Rimmon A beacon hill. 3/19

Minalcor Romendacil *Q* (Glorious Tower Eastvictor). The eighteenth King of Gondor. **minas** = tower, **alcar** = glory, **romen** = east, **dacil** = victor. 3/319

Minardil *Q* (Devoted to the Towers). The twenty-fourth King of Gondor. **minas** = tower, **dil** = lover of, devoted to. 3/319

minas 'tower'. S/361

Minas Anor *S* 'Tower of the Setting Sun'. The original name of Minas Tirith. **minas** = tower, **anor** = sun. 1/257

Minas Ithil *S* 'Tower of the Rising Moon'. The original name of Minas Morgul. **minas** = tower, **ithil** = moon. 1/257

Minas Morgul 'Tower of Sorcery'. The name of Minas Ithil after its capture by the Witch King. **minas** = tower, **morgul** = sorcery. 1/258

Minas Tirith *S* 'Tower of Watch', 'Tower of Guard'. The watch tower built by Finrod, later taken by Sauron. **minas** = tower, **tir** = watch. S/120

Minas Tirith *S* 'Tower of Watch', 'Tower of Guard'. The royal city of Gondor. 1/258

Minastan *Q* (Exalted Tower). The twenty-fifth King of Gondor. **minas** = tower, **tan** = high, exalted. 3/318

Mindeb A river tributary to the Sirion. S/121

Mindolluin 'Towering Blue-Head'. The mountain above Minas Tirith. **min** see **minas** = tower, **dol** = head, **luin** = blue. 3/23

Mindon Eldaliéva 'Lofty Tower of the Eldalië'. Ingwë's

tower in Tirion. **min** see **minas** = tower, **don** = lofty, **eldalië** = Elves, **-eva** = of. S/59

Minhiriath *S* 'Between the Rivers'. The land between the Baranduin and the Gwathlo. **hir** from **sir** = river, **-ath** = collective plural suffix. 1/00.

minno *S* 'enter'. 1/319

minuial *S* 'marrowdim', 'morning twilight'. See entry **min.** This element may be used to indicate the *rising* of the sun. **uial** = twilight. 3/389

minya *Q* 'first'. S/361

mîr *S* 'jewel'. S/361

mírë *Q* 'jewel'. S/361

miri *Q* 'jewels'. R/59

míriel *S* 'sparkling like jewels'. R/64

Míriel *Q* (Sparkling Jewel). The mother of Fëanor. S/60

miruvor *Q* 'nectar'. Compare **mírë** = jewel. R/58

miruvoreva *Q* 'nectar of'. R/58

mith *S* 'gray'. S/362

Mitheithel *S* 'Hoarwell'. A river in Eriador. **mith** = gray, **eithel** = spring, well. 1/212

Mithlond *S* 'Gray Haven'. **mith** = gray, **lond** = haven, harbor. 3/310

Mithrandir *S* 'Gray Pilgrim'. The Elvish name of Gandalf. **mith** = gray, **randir** = wanderer, from **ran** = wander. 1/374

mithril *S* (gray brilliance). Truesilver, Moria-silver. **mith** = gray, **ril** = brilliance. 1/248

Mithrim *S* (Gray Host). The name of a people of the Sindarin Elves, later given to a lake and the region around it where they dwelt. **mith** = gray, **rim** = host. S/106

mor 'dark'. Sometimes translated 'black'. S/362

Morannon *S* 'Black Gate'. The entrance to Mordor.

mor = dark, **annon** = large gateway. 1/244

morchaint *S* 'dark shapes'. Shadows cast by light as contrasted with dimness. S/359

Mordor *S* (Dark Country). Sauron's realm after the First Age. **mor** = dark, **dor** = land. 1/52

Morgai (Dark Points). The inner ridge of Mordor. **mor** = dark, **ae** = point. 3/175

Morgoth *Q* 'The Black Enemy'. The name Fëanor gave to the Vala Melkor. **mor** = dark, **goth** = enemy. 3/314

Morgul 'Black Arts', 'Sorcery'. **mor** = dark, **gul** = sorcery, from the root **ngol** = knowledge. 1/266

Morgulduin (River of Sorcery). The river that flows through Imlad Morgul. **morgul** = black arts, **duin** = river. 2/306

Moria 'Black Pit', 'Black Chasm'. Caverns where Dwarves lived and mined until they loosed the Balrog which gave the place its evil name. **mor** = dark, **ia** = abyss. 1/253

Moriquendi 'Elves of the Darkness'. The Elves who never saw the light of the Two Trees. **mor** = dark, **quendi** = Elves, literally 'speakers'. S/53

morimaitesincahonda *Q* A description of Orcs made by Treebeard. **mor** = dark, **maite** = hand. 3/257

Mormegil 'The Black Sword'. A name of Túrin. **mor** = dark, **megil** = sword. S/210

mornië *Q* 'darkness'. R/59

Morthond 'Blackroot'. The river that issues from the Paths of the Dead into Gondor. **mor** = dark, **thond** = root. 3/43

Morwen (Dark Maiden). The mother of Túrin and Nienor, wedded to Húrin. **mor** = dark, **wen** = maiden. S/148

Morwen (Dark Maiden) called 'Steelsheen'. The woman

from Lossarnach who wedded Thengel of Rohan. 3/351

moth 'dusk'. S/362

Mûmak 'Oliphaunt'. The great war-elephants of Harad. Compare *mammoth.* 2/269

Mumakil 'Oliphaunts'. 3/101

mundo *Q* 'bull'. T/240

Muzgâsh *B* An Orc. **ghâsh** = fire. 3/182

N

na *Q* 'is'. R/59

Nahar The horse of the Vala Oromë. Named for the sound of its neighing. S/29

nai *Q* 'be it that', 'may it be that'. R/59

nainië *Q* 'lament'. R/58

Naith The Gore or Tongue of Lórien, the angle of land at the meeting of the Celebrant and the Anduin. 1/361

nalda T/76.

nallon *S* 'I cry'. R/64

namárië *Q* 'farewell'. R/55

Námo 'Judge', 'Ordainer'. The Vala called Mandos. S/24

nan(d) 'valley'. S/362

Nan-Curunír 'Wizard's Vale,' 'Vale of Saruman'. The circular valley at the end of the Misty Mountains where Saruman lived in the tower of Isengard. **nan** = valley, **Curunír** = Saruman, literally 'Man of Skill'. 2/90

Nan Dungortheb 'Valley of Dreadful Death'. The valley between Doriath and Ered Gorgoroth. **nan** = valley, **gurth** = death. S/81

Nan Elmoth (Valley of Star-dusk). The forest where Thingol met Melian. **nan** = valley, **el** = star, **moth** = dusk. S/55

Nan Tasarion *Q* 'Willow Vale' where the rivers Narog

and Sirion meet. **nan** = valley, **tasarë** = *Q* willow, *S* **tathar, -ion** = place name suffix. 2/72

Nan Tathren *S* 'Willow Vale,' 'Land of Willows.' *S* name of Nan Tasarion. S/120

Nandor 'Those Who Turn Back'. The Elves of the Teleri who refused to come west beyond the Misty Mountains. S/54

Nanduhirion 'Dimrill Dale'. The valley east of Moria containing the Mirrormere. **nan** = valley, **du** = dimness, **hir** from **sir** = stream, **-ion** = place name suffix. 1/296

nár *Q* 'fire'. *S* **naur.** S/362

Narbeleth *S* 'sun-waning'. *Q* **narquellië.** The autumn season and the month corresponding to October. **anar** = sun. 3/386

Narchost (Fortress of Fire). One of the Towers of the Teeth in Mordor. **nar** = fire, **ost** = fortress. 3/176

Nardol (Fire-Head). A beacon hill. **nar** = fire, **dol** = head. 3/78

Nargothrond 'The Great Underground Fortress on the River Narog'. The fortress founded by Finrod Felagund. From **Narog-ost-rond. ost** = fortress, **rond** = vaulted hall. S/114

Narië *Q* (fiery). *S* **Norui.** The month corresponding to June. 3/388

Narmacil I *Q* (Sword of Fire). The sixteenth King of Gondor. **nar** = fire, **macil** see **megil** = sword. 3/319

Narmacil II *Q* (Sword of Fire). The twenty-eighth King of Gondor. 3/319

Narn i Hîn Húrin 'The Tale of the Children of Húrin'. **narn** = a tale in verse spoken rather than sung, **i** = the, **híni** = children. S/198

Narog The main river of West Beleriand. S/96

Narquellië *Q* (Sun-waning). *S* **Narbeleth.** The month corresponding to October. 3/388

Narsil 'red and white flame'. The sword of Elendil. **nar** = fire, **sil** = shine with a white or silver light. 1/256

Narsilion (red flame and white). The song of the sun and moon. **nar** = fire, **anar** = sun, **sil** = shine with a white or silver light, **isil** = moon. S/99

Narvi The Elven wright who made the west-doors of Moria. **nar** = fire 1/318

Narvinyë *Q*, *S* **Narwain.** The month corresponding to January. **nar** = fire, **anar** = sun. 3/388

Narwain *S*, *Q* **Narvinyë.** The month corresponding to January. 3/388

Narya 'Ring of Fire', 'The Red Ring'. Gandalf's Elven Ring. **nar** = fire. 3/310

naug *S* 'dwarf'. S/362

Nauglamir 'Necklace of the Dwarves'. Made by the Dwarves for Finrod. **naug** = dwarf, **mir** = jewel. S/114

Naugrim *S* 'The Stunted People'. Dwarves. **naug** = dwarf, **rim** = host. S/91

naur *S* 'fire'. S/362

nazg *B* 'ring'. 1/267

Nazgûl *B* 'Ringwraith'. **nazg** = ring, **gûl** = sorcery. 2/101

ndak 'battle'. The root for **dagor** = battle, **dagnir** = bane, and **dacil** = victor. S/357

ndor 'land'. The root for the Sindarin word **nor** = land. S/357

ndu 'down from on high'. S/355

(n)dur 'devotion', 'devoted to', 'friend', 'lover of'. A suffix to names. S/362

nef *S* 'on this side of'. R/64

Neithan 'The Wronged'. Literally 'one who is deprived'. A name of Túrin. S/200

neldë 'three'. S/362

neldor 'beech'. S/362

Neldoreth (Beech-land). A beech forest in Doriath. **neldor** = beech. 1/206

nen 'water'. S/362

Nen Echui *S* 'Water of Awakening'. A name of Cuivienen, the lake by which the Elves first awoke. **nen** = water, **echui** = awakening. S/357

Nen Girith 'Shuddering Water'. The falls of Celebros. **nen** = water, **girith** = shuddering. S/220

Nen Hithoel *S* (Lake of Mist). The lake above Rauros. **nen** = water, **hith** = mist. 1/384

Nénar (Water on High). A star. **nen** = water, **ar** = high, noble, royal. S/48

Nénimë *Q* (Watery). *S* **Ninui**. The month corresponding to February. **nen** = water, **-imë** = adjective suffix. 3/388

Nenning A river in West Beleriand. **nen** = water. S/120

Nenuial *S* 'Water of the Twilight'. Lake Evendim in northern Arnor. **nen** = water, **uial** = twilight. 3/389

Nenya 'The Ring of Water'. Galadriel's Elven Ring. **nen** = water. 1/380

Nerdanel The wife of Fëanor. **el** = star. S/64

Nessa A Vala, sister of Oromë, wedded to Tulkas. S/25

Nevrast 'Hither Shore'. A region south of the Firth of Drengist, west of Dor Lómin. **nev** = hither, see **nef** = on this side of, **rast** = shore. S/114

Ngaurhoth (werewolf-host). The wolves west of Moria that attacked the Fellowship. **gaur** = werewolf, **hoth** = host. 1/312

ngol 'lore', 'knowledge'. Ancient root from which were

derived **Noldor** = the Wise, and **gûl** = sorcery. S/359

Ngoldo (Wise). One of the Noldor, the name of a Quenya letter, probably *ng*. 3/401

ngwalme *Q* 'torment'. The name of a Quenya letter, probably *ngw*. 3/401

ngwaw 'howl'. S/359

nibin *S* 'petty'. S/362

Nienna 'Mourning'. A Vala, sister to Mandos and Lórien. S/28

Nienor 'Mourning'. The sister of Túrin. S/199

nil 'devoted to', 'lover of'. From **dil**. S/362

nim *S* 'white'. S/362

Nimbrethil (White Birch). Birchwoods in Arvernien. **nim** = white, **brethil** = birch. 1/256

Nimloth *S* 'White Flower'. The White Tree of Númenor. **nim** = white, **loth** = flower. 1/257

Nimloth *S* 'White Blossom'. The mother of Elwing, wedded to Dior. S/234

Nimphelos *S* (White Snow). A great pearl. **nimp** = white, **los** = snow. S/92

Nimrodel *S* 'Lady of the White Cave'. An Elven-maid of Lórien and the stream named for her. **nim** = white, **grod** = underground dwelling, **el** = Elf. 1/353

nin *Q* 'for me'. R/59

nîn 'wet'. S/362

Nindalf 'Wetwang'. Marshes on the Anduin below Rauros. **nin** = wet. 1/386

Níniel 'Tear Maiden'. A name of Nienor. **nin** = wet, **-iel** = feminine name suffix. S/344

ninque *Q* 'white'. S/362

Ninquelótë *Q* 'White Blossom'. A name of the White Tree. **ninque** = white, **lótë** = blossom. S/34

Nínui *S* (Watery) *Q* **Nenimë.** The month corresponding to February. **nîn** = wet, **-ui** = adjective suffix. 3/388

niphred 'pallor'. S/362

niphredil (pale point). The pale flowers which bloomed in Doriath when Lúthien was born and which also grew in Lórien. **niphred** = pallor, **dil** = point. 1/265, S/91

Nirnaeth Arnoediad 'Tears Unnumbered'. A battle of the Wars of Beleriand. S/138

Nivrim (Near-host). The part of Doriath on the western bank of the Sirion. **niv** see **nev** = hither, **rim** = host. S/122

noegyth *S* 'dwarves'. S/362

Noegyth Nibin 'Petty Dwarves'. Diminished Dwarves long banished from the great Dwarf-cities. S/204

nogoth *S* 'dwarf'. S/362

nogothrim *S* 'dwarf-folk'. R/67

Nogrod (Dwarf-delving). A Dwarf City in Ered Luin, called Hollowbold, and in Dwarvish called Tumunzahar. **nogoth** = dwarf, **grod** = delvings, underground dwellings, originally **Nov-rod** = hollow delving. 3/352

Noldo *Q* (Wise). One of the Noldor, the name of a Quenya letter, probably *ng*.

Noldor *Q* 'The Wise'. The Deep Elves. *S* **Golodh.** 3/44

Noldolantë *Q* 'The Fall of the Noldor'. A lament. **lantë** = fall. S/87

nólë *Q* 'long study', 'lore', 'knowledge'. S/357

Nom, Nomin *M* 'Wisdom', 'the Wise'. Names the Men under Beor's leadership gave to Finrod, **Nom,** and his people, **Nomin.** S/141

nor *Q* 'land'. From **nórë** 'people'. S/357

noro *S* 'ride'. Imperative verb. 1/225

Norui *S* (Sunny). *Q* **Nárië.** The month corresponding to June. **anor** = sun. 3/388

nostari In *A Vanimar, vanimálion, nostari*. 3/259

nov 'hollow'. S/359

Novrod 'Hollowbold'. The original name of Nogrod. **nov** = hollow, **rod** = delving. S/344

nu *Q* 'under'. R/58

Nulukkizdîn *K* The Dwarvish name for Nargothrond. S/230

numen *Q* 'west'. The name of the Quenya letter *n*. 3/401

Númenor *Q* 'Westernesse'. **numen** = west, **nor** = land. 1/206

Númenórë *Q* 'Westernesse'. **numen** = west, **nórë** = people. 3/406

nuquerna 'reversed'. 3/401

nur 'devotion', 'devoted to', 'friend', 'lover of'. S/362

Nurn (Dark). A plain in Mordor. 1/00.

Núrnen (Dark Water). The bitter inland sea in Mordor. **núr** from **dúr** = dark. 3/201

Nurtalë Valinóreva 'The Hiding of Valinor'. The concealment of Valinor from Morgoth. S/102

nwalmë *Q* 'torment'. The name of a Quenya letter, probably *ngw*. 3/401

O

o *S* 'from', 'of'. R/64

odo *S* 'seven'. S/364

Ohtar 'Warrior'. The squire of Isildur. 1/257

oi *Q* 'ever'. R/61

oialë *S* 'everlastingly'. R/59

oio *Q* 'everlastingly'. R/61

Oiolosse *Q* 'Everwhite'. The highest mountain in Valinor. **oio** = ever, **losse** = snow-white. 1/394

Oiolosseo *Q* 'Everwhite-from'. **-o** = from. R/61

Oiomúrë *Q* A region of mists near the Helcaraxe. **oio** = ever. S/80

Olog-Hai *B* Warrior Trolls. Compare **Torog** = troll. 3/401

Olorin Gandalf's name in the West in his youth, his name as a Maia. 2/279

olvar 'growing things with roots in the earth'. S/45

Olwë The brother of Elwë (Thingol), Lord of the Teleri of Alqualóndë in the Blessed Realm. S/53

oma-ryo *Q* 'voice-hers'. **oma** = voice, **ry** = her, **-o** = possessive suffix. R/57

omentielvo *S* (of our meeting). 1/90

-on *S* Augmentive suffix. R/65

ondo *Q* 'stone'. S/359

Ondoher *Q* (Lord of Stone). The thirtieth King of Gondor. **ondo** = stone, **her** = lord. 3/318

Ondolinde *Q* 'Stone Song'. The original name of Gondolin in Quenya. **ondo** = stone, **lin** = song. S/359

onen *S* 'I gave'. 3/342

Onod *S* (Ent). Plural **Enyd.** See following entry.

Onodrim *S* 'Ents'. The Shepherds of the Trees. **rim** = host. 2/45

or *S* (day). From **aur** = sunlight. S/365

Oraearon *S* 'Seaday'. *Q* **Earenya. or** = day, **aear** = sea, **-on** = augmentive suffix. 3/388

Oranor *S* 'Sunday'. *Q* **Anarya. or** = day, **anor** = sun. 3/388

Orbelain *S* 'Valarsday'. *Q* **Valanya. or** = day, **belain** = powers. 3/388

orch *S* 'goblin'. 3/409

Orcrist 'Goblin-Cleaver'. Thorin's sword. **orch** = goblin, **rist** = cleaver. 1/293

ore *Q* 'heart', 'inner mind'. The name of the Quenya letter weak *r*. 3/401

Orfalch Echor The ravine that made a gateway to Gondolin. **echor** = encircling wall. S/239

Orgaladh *S* 'Tree-Day'. *Q* **Aldea.** The day dedicated to the White Tree. **or** = day, **galadh** = tree. 3/388

Orgaladhad *S* 'Treesday'. *Q* **Alduya. or** = day, **galadh** = tree. 3/388

Orgilion *S* 'Starsday'. *Q* **Elenya. or** = day, **gili** = stars, **-on** = augmentive suffix. 3/388

Orithil *S* 'Moonday'. *Q* **Isilya. or** = day, **ithil** = moon. 3/388

Ormal (Uplifted Gold). The southern lamp of the Valar. **ortanë** = lifted up, **mal** = gold. S/35

Ormenel *S* 'Heavenday'. *Q* **Menelya. or** = day, **menel** = heaven. 3/388

orn *S* 'tree'. Plural **yrn.** S/362

Ornemalin (Golden Tree). Lothlórien. 2/70

Ornendil (Lover of Trees). The son of Eldacar. **orn** = tree, **dil** = friend, lover of. 3/327

Oro-mardi *Q* 'high halls'. **oro** = high, **mardi** from **mar** = home, dwelling. R/58

oro(d) *S* 'mountain'. Plural **ered.** S/362

Orod-na-Thôn (Pine Mountain). The forest of Dorthonion. **orod** = mountain, **thôn** = pine. 2/90

Orocarni 'The Red Mountains'. The mountains eastward in ancient Middle-earth. **orod** = mountain, **carne** = red. S/49

Orodreth A son of Finarfin. **orod** = mountain. S/61

Orodreth The sixteenth Ruling Steward of Gondor. 3/319

Orodruin 'The Mountain of Blazing Fire', 'The Burning Mountain'. Mount Doom. **orod** = mountain, **ruin** = red flame. 1/70

Orofarnë A rowan tree mourned by Bregalad. **oro** = high. 2/87

Oromë *Q* 'Horn-blowing', 'Sound of Horns'. *S* **Araw.** A

Vala. **rom** = an element representing the sound of trumpets. 3/112

Oromet (Last Mountain). A hill in western Numenor where the tower of Tar Minastir was built. **orod** = mountain, **met** = end, last. S/269

Orophin One of the Galadrim. **oro** = mountain. 1/357

ortanë *Q* 'lifted up'. R/58

Orthanc 'Mount Fang', 'Forked Height'. Saruman's tower. 2/160

Osgiliath 'Fortress of the Stars'. The abandoned royal city of Gondor on the Anduin. **ost** = fortress, **gili** = stars, **-ath** = collective plural suffix. R/56

Ossë A Maia of the sea. S/30

Ossir (Seven Rivers). The land of seven rivers in East Beleriand. **odo** = seven, **sîr** = river. 2/72

Ossiriand 'Land of the Seven Rivers'. See **Ossir. -iand** = place name suffix. 2/72, S/94

os(t) 'fortress'. S/362

Ost-in-Edhil "Fortress of the Eldar' in Eregion. **ost** = fortress, **in** = of the, **Edhil** = Elves. S/286

Ostgiliath "Fortress of the Stars'. A form of the name **Osgiliath**. R/65

Ostoher (Fortress Lord). The sixth King of Gondor. **ost** = fortress, **her** = lord. 3/318

otso *Q* 'seven'. S/362

P

palan *S* 'abroad', 'far-off', 'far-and-wide'. R/65

palan-diriel *S* 'gazing afar'. **diriel** = gazing. R/64

palantir *S* 'far-seer'. **palan** = far-off, **tir** = watch. 2/202

palantiri *S* 'far seers', 'that which looks far away'. The Seeing Stones. 2/202

parma *Q* 'book'. The name of the Quenya letter *p*. 3/401

parmatéma *Q* 'P-series'. The series of letters in the Quenya Tengwar alphabet starting with *p*. **parma** = book, **téma** = series. 3/401

parth 'sward', 'lawn'. S/356

Parth Galen 'Green Sward'. A lawn on the west side of Nen Hithoel above Rauros. **parth** = sward, **galen** = green. 1/411

pata 'way'. S/364

paur *S* 'fist', 'hand'. S/357

pedo *S* 'say', 'speak'. Imperative verb. 1/319

pel 'go around', 'encircle'. S/362

Pelargir 'Garth of Royal Ships'. A city on the Anduin. **pel** = encircle, **ar** = royal, **gir** from **cir** = ship. 3/62

Pelendur (Devoted to the Garth). A Steward of Gondor who ruled after the fall of Ondoher. The name may refer to the Fenced Lands of Minas Tirith. **pel** = encircle, **-dur** = devoted to, lover of. 3/319

Pelennor 'Fenced Land'. The walled townlands around Minas Tirith. **pel** = encircle, **nor** = land. 3/21

pella *Q* 'beyond the borders of'. **pel** = encircle. R/58

Pelori 'Fencing or Defensive Heights'. The encircling mountains of Valinor. **pel** = encircle, **oro** = high, mountain, **-i** = plural suffix. R/61

penna *S* 'slants down'. R/64

per (half). See following entries.

Peredhil 'Half-elven'. **per** = half, **edhil** = Elves. 3/314

periain 'Halflings'. Hobbits. **per** = half. R/67

perian 'Halfling'. Hobbit. 3/135

pharaz *N* (gold). 3/392

pherian *S* 'Halflings'. **pher** from **per** = half. R/67

pheriannath *S* 'Halflings'. **pher** from **per** = half, **-ath** = collective plural suffix. R/67

Phurunargian *C* The Common Speech name for Moria, Dwerrowdelf. 3/415

pilingeve T/76

pinnath *S* 'ridges'. -ath = collective plural suffix. S/356

Pinnath Gelin 'Green Ridges'. A land in fief to Gondor. **pinnath** = ridges, **gelin** = green (plural). 3/43

Poros A river in southern Gondor. **ros** = foam. 3/00.

pushdug *B* 2/59.

Q

quárë *Q* 'fist', 'hand'. S/357

quelle *Q* 'fading'. *S* **firith** The fourth season in the Elvish six-season year. 3/385

quen *Q* 'say', 'speak'. S/363

Quendi *Q* 'The Speakers', 'Those that speak with voices'. The original name for all Elves. 3/415

Quenta Silmarillion 'The History of the Silmarils'. S/286

Quenya (speech). The High Elven language. 3/405

quesse *Q* 'feather'. The name of the Quenya letter *q*. 3/401

quesse-téma *Q* 'Q-series'. The series of letters starting with *q* in the Quenya Tengwar alphabet. **quesse** = feather, **téma** = series. 3/401

quet *Q* 'say', 'speak'. S/363

quetta *Q* 'word'. S/363

R

Radbug *O, B* An Orc. 3/182

Radhruin (Street of Red Flame). A companion of Barahir. **radh** compare **rath** = street, **ruin** = red flame. S/155

raen 'wander', 'stray'. S/363

Ragnor A companion of Barahir. S/155

rais *S* 'horns'. S/363

ram *S* 'wall'. S/363

rama *Q* 'wing'. R/58

ramar *Q* 'wings'. R/58

ramba *Q* 'wall'. S/363

Ramdal 'Wall's End'. The end of the cliff that divided Beleriand. **ram** = wall, **dal** = foot. S/122

Rammas Echor 'Great Wall of the Outer Circle'. The outwall of the Pelennor. **ram** = wall, **echor** = encircle. 3/22

ran 'wander', 'stray'. S/363

Rána 'The Wanderer'. A name of the moon. S/99

randir (wanderer). See **Aerandir** 'Sea-wanderer', **Mithrandir** 'Gray Pilgrim'.

rant 'course'. S/363

ranu *H* A group of cottages. 3/416

Ranugad *H* 'Stay-at-Home', 'Hamfast'. 3/416

ras *S* 'horn'. S/363

rast (shore). See **Nevrast** 'Hither Shore', **Andrast** (Long Coast).

rath (street). See following entries.

Rath Celerdain 'Lampwright's Street'. **rath** = street, **dain** = wright. 3/40

Rath Dínen 'Silent Street'. The road to the tombs of Minas Tirith. **rath** = street, **dín** = silent. 3/100

Rathlóriel 'Golden Bed'. The name of the river Ascar after the treasure of Doriath was sunk there. **rath** = street, **lor** = golden. S/123

raug *S* 'demon'. S/363

rauko *Q* 'demon'. S/363

Rauros 'Roaring Spray'. The falls on the border of Gondor. **ros** = spray, foam. 1/384

ré 'day'. 3/385

réd (heir). See **Eluréd** 'Heir of Elu'.

Region (Land of Holly). A forest in the south of Doriath. **ereg** = holly, thorn, **-ion** = place name suffix. S/55

rem *Q* 'mesh'. 3/393

remb *Q* 'mesh'. 3/393

rembre *Q* 'mesh'. 3/393

Remmirath 'The Netted Stars'. Probably the Pliades. **rem** = mesh, **mir** = jewel, **-ath** = collective plural suffix. 1/91

Rerir A mountain north of Lake Helevorn. S/112

rest (shore). See **rast** = (shore) and **Eglarest,** a haven.

rhîw *S* 'winter'. *Q* **hrívë**. The fifth of the six Elvish seasons. 3/386

Rhosgobel Radagast's home near Mirkwood. **rhos** from **ros** = foam, **bel** = powers. 1/269

Rhovanion Wilderland east of the Misty Mountains. 3/344

Rhudaur Northeastern Arnor. **rhûn** = east. 3/320

rhûn *S* 'east'. 3/401

Rhûn *S* 'east'. The eastern lands. 1/261

Rían Wife of Huor, mother of Tuor. S/148

riel *Q* 'garlanded maiden'. From **rig.** S/360

rig 'twine', 'wreathe'. S/360

ril 'brilliance'. S/363

rildë *Q* 'brilliance'. S/363

rillë *Q* 'brilliance'. S/363

rim *S* 'great number', 'host', collective plural suffix. S/363

rimbë *Q* 'great number', 'host', collective plural suffix. S/363

rín (remembrance). See **Elurín** 'Remembrance of Elu'.

ring 'cold', 'chill'. S/363

Ringarë *Q* (Cold Day). *S* **Girithron.** The month corresponding to December. **ring** = cold, chill, **arë** = sunlight. 3/388

Ringil (Cold Star). The sword of Fingolfin. **ring** = cold, chill, **il** from **el** = star. S/153

Ringlo A river in Gondor. **ring** = cold, chill. 3/43

Ringwil (Cold Sky). A stream flowing into the Narog. **ring** = cold, chill, **wilya** = sky. S/122

ris 'cleave'. S/363

Rivil A stream flowing north from Dorthonion. S/191

roch *S* 'horse'. S/363

Rochallor (Golden Horse). The horse of Fingolfin. **roch** = horse, **lor** = golden. S/153

Rochand 'Riddermark'. A form of the name **Rohan. roch** = horse. 3/393

Rochann 'Riddermark'. A transitional form of the name **Rohan. roch** = horse. 3/393

rod *S* 'cave', 'underground dwelling', 'delving'. S/359

rod *S* (powers). See following entry.

Rodyn *S* 'Powersday'. *Q* **Tárion.** 3/388

rog *S* 'demon'. S/363

ro(h) *S* 'horse'. S/363

Rohan 'Riddermark'. The land of the Rohirrim north of Gondor. **ro** = horse. 3/393

Roheryn 'Horse of the Lady'. Aragorn's horse, a gift from Arwen. **ro** = horse, **hiril** = lady. 3/51

Rohirrim 'Masters of Horses'. The people of Rohan. **ro** = horse, **hir** = lord, **rim** = host. 1/275

rokko *Q* 'horse'. S/363

rom An element representing the sound of trumpets and horns. S/363

Romello *Q* 'East-from'. **rómen** = east, **ello** = from, of. R/59

rómen *Q* 'east', 'uprising', 'sunrise'. The name of the Quenya letter *r*. 3/401

Rómendacil *Q* 'East-Victor'. The title taken by the kings of Gondor who were victorious over the Easterlings. **rómen** = east, **dacil** = victor. 3/324

Romenna (East Númenor). A harbor on the east coast of Númenor. **rómen** = east, **Elenna** = a name of Númenor. S/265

rond 'vaulted or arched roof, or a hall or chamber so roofed'. S/363

ros 'foam', 'spindrift', 'spray'. S/363

roth (foam). Compare **ros.** See following entry.

Rothinzil *N* 'Foamflower'. The Númenorean name of Eärendil's ship, Vingilot. S/259

rûdh (bald). See **Amon Rûdh** 'Bald Hill'.

ruin *S* 'red flame'. S/364

Rúmil An inventor of a system of Tenqwar used only in Eldamar. 3/395

Rúmil One of the Gladrim. 1/357

rúnya *Q* 'red flame'. S/364

rúth 'anger'. S/364

S

Saeros A chief counsellor to Thingol. **ros** = foam. S/119

Salmar A Maia allied with the Vala Ulmo. S/40

Sammath Naur 'Chambers of Fire'. In Mount Doom. **-ath** = collective plural suffix, **naur** = fire. 3/219

sanga *Q* 'press', 'throng'. S/364

Sangahyando 'Throng-cleaver'. A leader of the Corsairs of Umbar. **sanga** = throng. 3/328

sarn 'small stone'. S/364

Sarn Ford 'Stone'. A ford on the Brandywine. 1/184

Sarn Athrad 'Ford of Stones' where the Dwarf-road crossed the river Gelion. **sarn** = stone, **thrad** = across. S/92

Sarn Gebir (Stone-Stakes). The rapids on the Anduin above the Argonath. 1/384

saur *Q* 'abominable', 'abhorrent'. S/364

Sauron *Q* 'The Abhorred'. The Dark Lord, originally a Maia serving Aulë. 1/24

Serech A marsh on the river Rivel. S/107

sereg *S* 'blood'. S/364

seregon *S* 'Blood of Stone'. A red-flowered plant growing on Amon Rûdh. **sereg** = blood, **gon** = stone. S/203

Serindë 'The Broideress'. A name of Míriel, mother of Fëanor. S/348

serkë *Q* 'blood'. S/364

Serni (Stones). A river in Gondor. **sarn** = stone. 3/00.

sha *B* 2/59

Shagrat *B* Captain of the Orcs of the Tower of Cirith Ungol. 2/344

Sharkú *B* 'old man'. The name the Orcs gave **Saruman, Sharkey**. 3/298

si *Q* 'now'. R/58

si *S* 'here'. R/64

sil *Q* 'shine with white or silver light'. S/364

sila 'shines'. 1/90

silima The light-enclosing crystal Fëanor devised for the Silmarils. R/64

silivren *S* 'white glittering'. R/64

Silmarien (Dwelling of White Light). Tar-Elendil's daughter. **sil** = shine with a white or silver light, **mar** = home, dwelling, **-ien** = feminine name suffix. 3/316

Silmaril *Q* (white-shining radiance). A jewel wrought by

Fëanor containing the light of the Two Trees. **sil** = shine, **ril** = radiance. 1/206

Silmarilli *Q* (white shining radiance). The three jewels. 3/313

Silmarillion *Q* The tale of the First Age and the silmarilli. 3/314

silme *Q* 'starlight'. The name of the Quenya letter *s*. 3/401

Silpion *Q* (The White-shining). A name of the White Tree. **sil** = shine with a white or silver light, **-ion** = masculine name suffix. S/38

sinda *Q* 'gray'. S/365

sindanoriello *Q* 'gray-country-from'. **sinda** = gray, **nori** = lands, **-ello** = from. R/59

Sindar *Q* 'Gray-Elves'. The Elves of the Twilight in Beleriand, under Thingol's leadership. **sinda** = gray, **-r** = plural suffix. 3/415

Sindarin *S* 'Gray Elven'. 3/405

Sindarinwa *Q* 'Gray-Elven'. 3/401

singe T/76.

Singollo *Q* 'Graycloak', 'Gray-Mantle'. Also **Sindacollo**, the Quenya name of Thingol. **sinda** = gray, **collo** = cloak. S/365

sinome *Q* 'in this place'. See **si** = here. 3/245

sîr 'river'. S/364

sir 'flow'. S/364

Sirannon 'Gatestream'. The stream running down from the west-doors of Moria. **sir** = stream, **annon** = gate. 1/314

Sirion 'The Great River' which divided East and West Beleriand. **sir** = river, **-on** = augmentive suffix. S/51

Siriondil *Q* (Lover of the River). The tenth King of Gondor. **sir** = river, **dil** = friend, lover of. 3/318

sirith 'a flowing'. S/364

Sirith (The Flowing). A river in Gondor, tributary to the Anduin. 3/00.

skai *B* 2/59

snaga *B* 'slave'. 3/409

soron *Q* 'eagle'. S/365

Soronúmë *Q* A constellation. **soron** = eagle. S/48

sûl 'wind'. S/364

súle *Q* 'spirit'. A name for the Quenya letter *th.* Note the comparison, common to many languages, of spirit to wind, air, or breath. 3/401

Súlime *Q* (Windy). *S* **Gwaeron.** The month corresponding to March. **sûl** = wind, **-ime** = adjective suffix. 3/388

Súlimo 'Lord of the Breath of Arda'. Literally 'The Breather'. A title of Manwë the Elder King as Lord of Air. S/26

súrinen *Q* 'winds-in'. R/58

suyer T/76.

Súza *H* The Shire. 3/413

T

tal 'foot'. S/364

talan A flet (which means 'floor' or 'dwelling'). A platform in a tree such as the Galadrim used. 1/357

talath 'flat lands', 'plain'. S/364

Talath Dirnen 'The Guarded Plain' north of Nargothrond. **talath** = plain, **dir** = watch. S/147

Talath Rhûnen 'The East Vale'. A name of Thargelion. **talath** = plain, **rhûn** = east. S/124

Taniquetil 'High White Peak'. The highest mountain of Valinor. **tan** compare **ortanë** = lifted up, **que** compare **ninque** = white, **til** = point. R/61

tar *S* 'high'. S/364

tara *Q* 'lofty'. S/364

Tar-Alcarin *Q* (Glorious King). The seventeenth Monarch of Númenor. **alcarin** = glorious. 3/315

Tar-Amandil *Q* (Lover of Aman). The third Monarch of Númenor. **dil** = friend, lover. 3/315

Tar-Anárion *Q* (Sun King). The eighth Monarch of Númenor. **anár** = sun, **-ion** = masculine name suffix. 3/315

Tar-Ancalimë *Q* (Queen of Long Light). The first Queen and seventh Monarch of Númenor. **an** = long, **cal** = shine. 3/315

Tar-Ancalimon *Q* (King of Long Light). The fourteenth Monarch of Númenor. 3/315

Tar-Atanamir *Q* (Man of Jewels). The thirteenth Monarch of Númenor. **atan** = man, **mir** = jewel. 3/315

Tar-Calion *Q* (Heir of Light). The Quenya name of Ar-Pharazon, the twenty-fourth and last Monarch of Númenor. **cal** = shine, **-ion** = masculine name suffix translated as 'son', 'heir of'. S/270

Tar-Calmacil *Q* (Shining Sword). The eighteenth Monarch of Númenor. **cal** = shine, **megil** = sword. 3/315

Tar-Ciryatan *Q* 'The Shipbuilder'. The twelfth Monarch of Númenor. **cirya** = sharp-prowed ship. **tan** from **dan** = wright. 3/315

Tar-Elendil *Q* 'Elf-friend', 'Star-lover'. The fourth Monarch of Númenor. **elen** = star, **dil** = friend, lover. 3/315

Tar-Meneldur *Q* (Devoted to Heaven). The fifth Monarch of Númenor. **menel** = heaven, **dur** = lover of, devoted to. 3/315

Tar-Minastir *Q* (Watchtower). The eleventh Monarch of Númenor. **minas** = tower, **tir** = watch. 3/315

Tar-Minyatur *Q* (First Master). The royal name of Elros

Halfelven as first Monarch of Númenor. **minya** = first, **tur** = mastery. 3/315

Tar-Míriel *Q* (Jewel-Maiden). The daughter of Tar-Palantir. Her rule was usurped by Ar-Pharazôn. **mir** = jewel, **-iel** = feminine name suffix. 3/315

Tar-Palantir *Q* 'The Farsighted'. The twenty-third Monarch of Númenor. **palantir** = far-seer. 3/315

Tar-Súrion *Q* (King of the Wind). The ninth Monarch of Númenor. **sur** see **surinen** = wind-in, **-ion** = masculine name suffix. 3/315

Tar-Telemmaite *Q* (Last Hand). The fifteenth Monarch of Númenor. **tel** = end, be last, **maite** = hand. 3/315

Tar-Telperien *Q* (Silver Maiden). The second Queen, seventh Monarch of Númenor. **telpe** = silver, **-ien** = maiden, feminine name suffix. 3/315

Tar-Vanimelde *Q* The third Queen, sixteenth Monarch of Númenor. **vana** = fair, **mel** = love. 3/315

Tarannon Falastur (Gate King). 'Lord of the Coasts'. The eleventh King of Gondor. **tar** = king, **annon** = gate, **falas** = coast, **tur** = mastery, lord. 3/318

Taras (High Horn). A mountain on the Nevrast. **tar** = high, **ras** = horn. S/119

Tarcil *Q* (Númenorean). The seventh King of Arnor. **tarkil** = one of Númenorean descent. 3/318

Tarciryan *Q* (Ship-King). The father of Eärnil I. **tar** = king, **cirya** = sharp-prowed ship. 3/318

Tareldar *Q* (High Elves). **tar** = high, **Eldar** = Elves. S/326

Targon (High Commander). A man of Minas Tirith. **tar** = high, **gon** = commander. 3/35

Tári *Q* 'she that is lofty', 'queen'. R/58

tárienna In *Cormacolindor, a laite tárienna!* 3/231

Tarion *Q* 'Powersday'. *S* **Rodyn** see **tur** = power. 3/388

tark *C* 'man of Gondor'. Derived from **tarkil.** 3/409

tarkil *Q* 'one of Númenorean descent'. 3/409

Tarlang (High Iron). Tarlang's Neck, a pass above Lamedon. **tar** = high, **anga** = iron. 3/63

tarma 'pillar'. S/364

Tarmenel (High Heaven). In 'a wind of power in Tarmenel'. **tar** = high, **menel** = heaven. 1/247

Tarn Aeluin (Blue Point). A lake in Dorthonion. **Tarn** is probably the English word, a mountain lake. **ae** = point, **luin** = blue. S/162

Tarondor (Great King of the Land). The eighth King of Arnor. **tar** = king, **-on** = augmentive suffix, **dor** = land. 3/318

Tarostar Romendacil *Q* (King of Fortresses). 'East-Victor'. The seventh King of Gondor. **tar** = king, **ostar** = fortresses or royal fortress, **romen** = east, **dacil** = victor. 3/318

tasarë *Q* 'willow'. S/364

Tasarinan *Q* (Willow Vale). The Quenya name of Nantathren. **tasarë** = willow, **nan** = valley. 2/72

tathar *S* 'willow'. S/364

tathren *S* 'willow'. S/364

taur *S* 'wood', 'forest'. S/364

Taur e-Ndaedelos 'Forest of Great Fear'. Mirkwood. **taur** = forest, **dae** = shadow, **deloth** = abhorrence. 3/412

Taur-en-Faroth (Forest of the Hunters). The forested highland above Nargothrond. **taur** = forest, **en** = of, **faroth** = hunters. S/114

Taur-im-Duinath *S* 'the Forest between Rivers' between the Sirion and Gelion. **taur** = forest, **im** see **imbe** = between, **duin** = large river, **-ath** = collective plural suffix. S/123

Taur-na-Neldor (Beech Forest). A name of Neldoreth. **taur** = forest, **neldor** = beech. 2/72

Taur-nu-Fuin 'Forest under Night'. The later name of Dorthonion. **taur** = forest, **nu** = under, **fuin** = darkness. S/155

taurë *Q* 'forest'. S/364

Taurelilómëa *Q* 'Forest-many-shadowed'. A description of Fangorn Forest. **taurë** = forest, **lómë** = dusk. 3/409

Tauremorna *Q* (Dark Forest). Fangorn Forest. **taurë** = forest, **mor** = dark. 2/72

Tauremornalómë *Q* (Forest of Black Dusk). Fangorn Forest. **taurë** = forest, **mor** = dark, black, **lómë** = dusk. 2/72

Tauron 'The Forester', 'Lord of Forests'. A name among the Sindarin Elves for the Vala Oromë. **taur** = forest. S/29

te *Q* (them). 3/231

tehta *Q* 'sign'. The vowel signs used in Elvish script. 3/399

tehtar *Q* 'signs'. The vowel signs used in Elvish script. 3/397

Teiglin A river tributary to the Sirion. **glin** = gleam. S/120

teithant *S* (drew). 1/319

tel 'finish', 'end', 'be last'. S/364

Telchar The Dwarf-smith of Nogrod who wrought Andúril. **tel** = last. 2/115

telco 'stem'. The upright stroke of a Tengwar letter. 3/398

Telcontar *Q* 'Strider'. The Quenya name of the Royal House of Elessar (Aragorn). 3/139

telep *Q* 'silver'. S/357

Telemnar *Q* The twenty-fifth King of Gondor. **tel** = last. 3/319

Teleri 'Lastcomers', 'Hindmost'. The third people of Elves to come into Beleriand. **tel** = last. S/41

tellumar *Q* 'domes'. R/58

telpë *Q* 'silver'. S/357

Telperinquar *Q* (Silver Hand). The Quenya name of Celebrimbor. **telperin** = silver-like, **quar** = hand, fist. S/357

Telperion *Q* (Silver). The White Tree. **telpë** = silver, **-ion** = masculine name suffix. 3/250

Telumehtar *Q* (Swordsman of the Dome [of Heaven]). The constellation corresponding to Orion. **telluma** = dome, **mehtar** from **megil** = sword. 3/391

Telumehtar Umbardacil *Q* (Swordsman of the Dome, Victor of Umbar). The twenty-seventh King of Gondor. **dacil** = victor. 3/319

Telumendil *Q* (Devoted to the Dome of Heaven, Point of the Dome). A constellation. **telluma** = dome, **dil** = point, **-dil** = lover of, devoted to. S/48

téma *Q* 'series'. 3/397

témar *Q* 'series'. Plural. 3/398

Tengwar *Q* 'letters' of the Elvish script alphabet. 3/397

tenn' *Q* 'unto'. 3/245

thalion 'strong', 'dauntless'. S/364

Thalion 'Steadfast', 'Strong'. A name of Húrin. S/350

Thalos (Strong One of the Seven). One of the Seven Rivers of Ossiriand. **thalion** = strong, **os** from **otso** = seven. S/123

thang *S* 'oppression'. S/364

Thangorodrim *S* 'Mountains of Oppression'. The land of Morgoth. **thang** = oppression, **orod** = mountain, **rim** = host. 1/256

thar *S* 'athwart', 'across'. S/364

Tharbad (Across-way). A ford and ruined town on the Gwathlo. **thar** = across, **bad** = way. 1/287

Thargelion 'The Land beyond Gelion' where Caranthir dwelt. **thar** = across. S/124

Tharkûn *K* The name the Dwarves gave Gandalf. 2/279

thaur 'abominable', 'abhorrent'. S/364

Thauron 'The Abhorred'. A form of the name **Sauron.** S/364

thil *S* 'shine with a white or silver light'. S/364

thin(d) *S* 'gray'. S/365

Thingol *S* 'Graycloak'. The Elvenking of Doriath. **thin** = gray, **gol** = cloak. 1/206

thiw *S* (signs). 1/319

thôl *S* 'helm'. S/365

thôn *S* 'pinetree'. S/365

thond *S* 'root'. 3/393

thor (torrent). See **Brilthor** 'Glittering Torrent'.

thoron *S* 'eagle'. S/365

Thorondir *S* (Eagle-gaze). The twenty-second Ruling Steward of Gondor. **thoron** = eagle, **dir** = gaze. 3/319

Thorondor 'King of Eagles'. *Q* **Sorontar.** An eagle of the Encircling Mountains around Gondolin. **thoron** = eagle, **dor** = king, lord. 3/226, S/110

Thorongil *S* 'Eagle of the Star'. The name under which Aragorn rode with the Rohirrim and lived as a great captain in Gondor. **thoron** = eagle, **gil** = star. 3/335

thrad *S* 'across'. S/364

thrakatulûk *B* 'to bring them all'. 1/267

Thranduil (Halls of Star-Shadow). The King of the Elves of Mirkwood. **thrond** = hall, **du** = shadow, **il** from **el** = star. 1/253

thrond 'a hall or chamber with a vaulted roof'. S/363

thúle *Q* 'spirit'. A name for the Quenya letter *th*. 3/401

Thuringwethil 'Woman of Secret Shadow' who took bat-form as Sauron's messenger. **weth** = shadow. S/178

tier *Q* 'roads'. R/59

til 'point', 'horn'. S/365

Tilion 'The Horned'. The Maia who sails the moon. **til** = horn. S/99

tin *S* 'sparkle'. S/365

tinco *Q* 'metal'. The name of the Quenya letter *t*. 3/401

tinco-téma *Q* 'T-series'. The series of letters starting with *t* in the Quenya Tengwar alphabet. **téma** = series. 3/398

tindome *Q* 'starfading'. **tin** = star, **dōmē** = dimness. 3/389

tindomerel *Q* 'daughter of the twilight'. A poetic name for the nightingale. *S* **Tinuviel**. **tin** = star, **dōmē** = dimness. S/365

tinta *Q* 'cause to sparkle'. S/365

Tintalle *Q* 'Kindler', 'Star-kindler'. *S* **Gilthoniel**. A title of Varda as creator of the nearer stars. **tinta** = cause to sparkle. R/58

tintilar *Q* 'twinkle'. Plural. **tin** = sparkle. R/58

Tinuviel *S* 'Nightingale', 'Daughter of the Twilight'. Lú-thien of Doriath. **tin** = star, sparkle, **du** = dimness, **-iel** = daughter. 1/205

tinwe *Q* 'spark'. R/65

tir *S* 'watch over', 'look toward'. R/65

Tirion 'Great Watch Tower' in Elvenhome. **tir** = watch, **-on** = augmentive suffix. R/64

tiro *S* 'watch over'. Imperative verb. R/65

Tirith Aear *S* 'Seaward Tower'. **tirith** = watching, **aear** = sea. A/338

Tîw *S* 'Letters'. *Q* **Tengwar**. 3/385

tol 'island'. The word for sheer-sided islands either in rivers or in the sea. S/365

Tol Brandir *S* The Tindrock, the island in Nen Hithoel above Rauros. **tol** = island, **dir** = watch. 1/389

Tol Eressëa 'The Lonely Isle' standing off the shore of Elvenhome. **tol** = island, **er** = one, alone. S/50

Tol Galen 'The Green Isle' where Lúthien and Beren dwelt in Ossiriand after their return from death. **tol** = island, **galen** = green. S/123

Tol-in-Gaurhoth 'Isle of Werewolves'. The name of Tol Sirion after its capture by Sauron. **tol** = island, **in** = of, **gaur** = werewolf, **hoth** = host. S/156

Tol Morwen (The Island of Morwen). The island remaining after the flooding of Beleriand, bearing the memorial stone of Morwen and her children Túrin and Nienor. **tol** = island. S/230

Tol Sirion (The Island of the Sirion). An island in the river Sirion. **tol** = island. S/114

Tolfalas (Island Coast). The bay, containing an island, at Anduin's mouth. **tol** = island, **falas** = coast. 3/00

Torech Ungol 'Shelob's Lair'. **ungol** = spider. 2/326

Torog *S* 'troll'. 3/410

Trahald *M* 'burrowing', 'worming in'. The actual name of Smeagol. 3/415

trahan *R* 'a burrow'. 3/415

tran *H* 'a burrow'. 3/415

tuilë *Q* 'spring'. *S* **ethuil**. The first of the six seasons in the Elvish year. 3/385

tuilérë *Q* (spring-day). The first of the three midsummer days. **tuilë** = spring, **ré** = day. 3/387

Tulkas A Vala of strength and prowess. S/25

tum *S* 'valley'. S/365

Tumbalemorna *Q* 'deep-valley-black'. Fangorn Forest.

tum = valley, **bale** compare **búlë** = deep in **lumbúlë** 'deep shadow', **mor** = black. 3/409

Tumbaletaurëa *Q* 'deep-valley-forested'. Fangorn Forest. **taur** = forest, **-ëa** = adjective suffix. 3/409

tumbo *Q* 'valley'. S/365

Tumhalad (Valley-plain). The valley between the rivers Ginglith and Narog. **tum** = valley, **lad** = plain. S/212

Tumladen 'The wide valley' in which stood the city of Gondolin. **tum** = valley, **lad** = plain. S/115

Tumladen 'the wide valley'. A small vale southwest of Minas Tirith. 3/36

Tumunzahar *K* The Dwarvish name for Nogrod. S/352

Túna The hill in Elvenhome where the Elven city Tirion stood. S/59

Tuor The son of Huor, a mortal wedded to Idril Celebrindal. 3/314

tur 'power', 'mastery'. S/365

Tûr Haretha (Haleth's Mound). The burial mound of Lady Haleth. **tûr** may be the singular of **tyrn** = barrows. S/147

Turamarth *S* 'Master of Doom'. Sindarin form of Túrin's title **Turambar. tur** = master, **amarth** = doom. S/355

Turambar *Q* 'Master of Doom'. A title of Túrin. **tur** = master, **ambar** = doom. S/217

Turambar *Q* 'Master of Doom'. The eighth King of Gondor. 3/318

Turgon *Q* (Master Commander). The Elven King of Gondolin, father of Idril Celbrindal. **tur** = master, **gon** from **kano** = commander. 1/284

Túrin (Master). A great hero and Elf-friend of the First Age. **tur** = mastery. 1/284

turun (mastered). S/223

tyeller *Q* 'grades'. 3/397

tyelpetéma (silver-series). A series of letters in the Quenya Tengwar alphabet. **telpe** = silver, **téma** = series. 3/398

Tyrn Gorthad The Barrow-Downs. **tyrn** = barrows, **gurth** = death. 3/321

U

ú *B.* 2/59

ú (not). See following entries.

ú-chebin *S* (not kept). 3/342

ú-nót-imë *Q* 'not-count-able'. R/58

Udûn *S. Q* **Utumno.** The first stronghold of Morgoth. The Balrog in Moria was thus called 'Flame of Udûn'. **dûn** from **tum** = valley. S/365

Udûn *S* A vale in Mordor named for Morgoth's first stronghold. 3/205

Ufthak *O, B.* An Orc. 2/350

Ugluk *O, B.* The commander of the Orcs of Isengard. 2/48

ui *S* (ever). See **Uilos** 'Everwhite'.

-ui *S* (adjective suffix). See **Vedui, Ered Lithui, Imloth Melui,** and **Fanuidhol.**

uial *S* 'twilight'. 3/389

Uilos *S* 'Everwhite'. *Q* **Oiolosse.** The highest mountain in Valinor. **ui** = ever, **los** = snow white. R/66

Uinen (Everwater). A Maia, Lady of the Seas, wedded to Osse. **ui** = ever, **nen** = water. S/30

-ûl *K* (of). See **Khuzdûl** = the Dwarvish language; **Fundinûl** = 'Son of Fundin'

Úlaire *S* (Unlight). An Elvish name of the Ringwraiths. **ú** = not, **laire** = summer, green. S/352

Uldor An Easterling, son of Ulfang. S/157

Ulfang A chieftain of the Easterlings. S/157

Ulfast An Easterling, son of Ulfang. S/157

Ulmo 'Pourer' or 'Rainer'. A Vala, Lord of the Waters. S/26

Ulumúri The horns of Ulmo whose music gives sea-longing. S/27

Ulwarth An Easterling, son of Ulfang. S/157

Úmanyar 'Those not of Aman'. The Elves who started west but did not reach Aman. **ú** = not, **yar** = plural suffix. S/53

Úmarth 'Ill-Fate'. The false name for his father given by Túrin. **ú** = not, **amarth** = doom, fate. S/210

umbar *Q* 'fate'. The name of the Quenya letter *b* or *mb*. 3/401

Umbar *PN* A bay and nation of corsairs in South Gondor. 2/267

Umbardacil *Q* (Victor of Umbar). The title of the king of Gondor who was victorious over the corsairs of Umbar. **dacil** = victor. 3/329

un-túpe *Q* 'down-roofs'. R/59

undomë *Q* 'star-opening'. **dōmē** = dimness. 3/389

Undomiel *Q* 'Evenstar'. Arwen Undomiel, daughter of Elrond and Celebrian. **undome** = star-opening, twilight, **-iel** = feminine name suffix. 3/251

undu-lávë *Q* 'down-licked'. R/59

ungol (spider). See **Cirith Ungol** 'Spider's Pass', **Torech Ungol** 'Shelob's lair', **Ungoliant, ungwe** 'spider-web'

Ungoliant The spider-monster, destroyer of the Two Trees, mother of Shelob. **ungol** = spider. 2/332

ungwe *Q* 'spider-web'. The name of the Quenya letter with the values *g, gw,* and *ngw.* 3/401

unque *Q* 'a hollow'. The name of the Quenya letter *nqu.* 3/401

ur 'heat', 'be hot'. Compare **aurë,** sunlight, day. S/365

úre *Q* 'heat'. The name of a Quenya letter for which no transliteration is given. 3/401

Urime *Q* (hot). *S* **Úrui** The month corresponding to August. 3/388

Urthel A companion of Barahir. **ur** = heat. S/155

Úrui *S* (hot). *Q* **Urime.** The month corresponding to August. 3/388

Uruk *B* 'Orc'. A goblin, particularly a large fighting Orc. 1/338

Uruk-hai *B* Large fighting Orcs. 2/179

Urulóki *Q* 'Fire-serpent'. Dragon. **ur** = heat, **lókë** = snake, serpent. S/116

utulie'n *Q* 'has come'. S/190

utulien *Q* 'I have come'. 3/245

Utumno The first stronghold of Morgoth. **tum** = valley. S/36

utúvienyes *Q* 'I have found it'. Aragorn Elessar's exclamation at finding the sapling of the White Tree. 3/250

uva *Q* (will). See **enquantuva** = will refill, **hiruva** = will find, **maruvan** = I will abide.

Uzbad *K* 'Lord'. 1/333

V

vagor *S* (swordsman). See **Menelvagor** = 'The Swordsman of the Sky'.

Vairë 'The Weaver'. A queen of the Valar wedded to the Vala Mandos. S/25

val *Q* 'power'. S/365

Vala *Q* 'The Power'. The angelic powers who took part in the shaping of the world. R/66

Valacar *Q* (Royal Power). The nineteenth King of Gondor. **vala** = power, **ar** = royal, high, noble. 3/318

Valacirca 'The Sickle of the Valar'. The constellation the Great Bear or Big Dipper. S/48

Valandil *Q* (Devoted to the Valar). The third King of Arnor. **dil** = lover of, devoted to. 3/318

Valandur *Q* (Devoted to the Valar). The eighth King of Arnor. **dur** = devoted to. 3/318

Valanya *Q* (Valar's day). *S* **Orbelain.** 3/388

Valaquenta *Q* 'Account of the Valar'. See **quen** = say, speak. S/23

Valar *Q* 'The Powers', 'Those with Power'. The angelic powers who took part in the shaping of the world. 3/314

Valaraukar *Q. S* **Balrog.** 'Demons of Might'. The Maia who had gone over into the service of Morgoth and become demons. Singular **Valarauko. vala** = power, **rauko** = demon. S/31

Valaróma (Horn of the Vala). The horn of Oromë the Huntsman of the Valar. **rom** = an element suggesting the sound of horns. S/29

Valier *Q* 'Queens of the Valar'. Singular **Valië.** S/25

Valimar *Q* 'The Dwelling of the Valar' in the Blessed Realm. **mar** = home, dwelling. R/61

Valinor (The Lands of the Valar) in the Blessed Realm. **nor** = land. R/62

Valmar *Q* 'Dwelling of the Valar'. **mar** = dwelling, home. R/62

Vána A queen of the Valar, sister of Yavanna and wedded to Oromë. S/25

vanimálion *Q* **vanya** = fair. 3/259

vanimar *Q* (fair-home). **vanya** = fair, **mar** = home, dwelling, 3/259

vanimelda *Q* **vanya** = fair, **mel** = love. 1/367

vanwa *Q* 'lost'. R/59

Vanyar *Q* 'The Fair'. The first Elves to come west, many of whom had fair hair. Singular **Vanya**. S/40

Varda *Q* 'The Exalted'. Elbereth Gilthoniel, Queen of the Valar, wedded to Manwe the Elder King. R/66

Vardamir *Q* (Jewel of Varda). The second Monarch of Númenor. **mir** = jewel. 3/315

Vardo *Q* 'Varda's'. **-o** = possessive suffix. R/58

Vása 'The Consumer'. The Noldor's name for the sun. S/99

ve *Q* 'as'. R/59

vedui *S* 'last'. I/222

V'ematte. T/76

Vidugavia *M* A King of Rhovannion. Actually a Gothic name of a god of the woods. 3/326

Vidumavi *M* The daughter of Vidugavia, wedded to Valacar. 3/326

vilya *Q* 'air', 'sky'. The name for a Quenya letter for which no transliteration is given. 3/401

Vilya *Q* 'The Ring of Air'. Elrond's Elven-ring, the most powerful of the three. 3/308

ving 'foam', 'spray'. S/365

Vingilot *Q* The full name is **Vingilótë**. 'Foam-flower'. Eärendil's ship. **ving** = foam, **lótë** = flower. S/246

Vinitharya *M* Eldacar's name in Rhovannion. 3/326

Vinyamar 'New Dwelling'. The house of Turgon in Nevrast. **mar** = dwelling. S/115

Vinyarion Hyarmendacil The twenty-second King of Gondor. As he was the grandson of Eldacar, Vinyarion may have been a name from Rhovannion, or *Q* **vinya** = new, **-ion** = son. **Hyarmendacil** = East-victor. 3/319

Víressë *Q* The month corresponding to April. *S* **Gwirith**. 3/388

vorn 'black'. S/360

Voronwë 'The Steadfast'. An Elven mariner from Gondolin. S/196

Vorondil (Lover of Steadfastness). A steward of Gondor. See **Voronwë, dil** = lover of, devoted to. 3/319

W

waith 'people', 'folk'. S/359

wath 'shadow', 'dimness'. S/359

wen (sheen). **Morwen** 'Steelsheen', **Eledhwen** 'Elfsheen'.

wen 'maiden'. S/365

weth 'shadow', 'dimness'. S/359

Wilwarin *Q* 'Butterfly'. A constellation, perhaps Cassiopea. S/48

wilya *Q* 'air', 'sky'. A form of **vilya.** 3/401

wing 'foam', 'spray'. S/365

Y

ya T/76

yanta *Q* 'bridge'. *S* **iant.** The name of the Quenya letter *y.* 3/401

yassen *Q* 'which-in'. Plural. R/59

Yavanna *Q* 'Giver of Fruits'. A queen of the Valar, wedded to Aulë. **yávë** = fruit, **anna** = gift. S/27

Yavannië *Q* (Giver of Fruits). *S* **Ivanneth.** The month corresponding to September. 3/388

yávë *Q* 'fruit'. S/365

yávië *Q* 'autumn', 'harvest'. *S* **iavas.** The third of the six Elvish seasons. **yávë** = fruit. 3/385

yáviérë *Q* (autumn day). The last of the three midsummer days. **yávië** = autumn, **ré** = day. 3/387

yé *Q.* In *Ye! Utúvienyes!* 3/250

yén *Q* 'year'. A long Elven year of 144 solar years. Plural **yéni.** 3/385

yestarë *Q* The first day of the year. **arë** = sunlight, day. 3/386

yrch *S* 'Orcs'. 1/359

yuldar *Q* 'draughts'. R/58

yulma *Q* 'cup'. R/58

ywalme *Q* 'torment'. 3/401

Z

Zaragamba *H* 'Oldbuck'. 3/416

Zirak-Zigal *K* The Silvertine, one of the three mountains over Moria. 1/296